THE
PROTOTYPE OF HAMLET
AND
OTHER SHAKESPEARIAN PROBLEMS

BY
WM. PRESTON JOHNSTON

"Look into the seed of time
And say which grains will grow and which will not."
—*Macbeth*, I, 3.

NEW YORK:
BELFORD COMPANY, PUBLISHERS
18–22 EAST 18TH STREET

Library of Congress Cataloging in Publication Data

Johnston, William Preston, 1831-1899.
  The prototype of Hamlet.

  Reprint of the 1890 ed.
  CONTENTS: How to study Shakespeare.--Macbeth.--The
significance of Hamlet. [etc.]
    1. Shakespeare, William, 1564-1616. Hamlet.
2. Shakespeare, William, 1564-1616. Macbeth.
I. Title.
PR2807.J6 1972   822.3'3   71-170819
ISBN 0-404-03595-7

Reprinted from the edition of 1890, New York
First AMS edition published in 1972
Manufactured in the United States of America

International Standard Book Number: 0-404-03595-7

AMS PRESS INC.
NEW YORK, N. Y.   10003

THE PROTOTYPE OF HAMLET

AMS PRESS
NEW YORK

TO MY WIFE,

MARGARET AVERY JOHNSTON,

WITH WHOSE ENCOURAGEMENT AND APPROVAL

THESE LECTURES WERE WRITTEN,

THIS BOOK

IS DEDICATED.

April 25th, 1890.

CONTENTS.

LECTURE FIRST.

HOW TO STUDY SHAKESPEARE.

The growth of literary aspiration. Definition of true literature : one form of the Church of God, holy, catholic and apostolic. Implicit moral culture of the drama. Shakespeare's popularity and hold upon the thought of the world. Advantages of Shakespeare as a study; interesting, stimulating to the reason and esthetic sense; the best aid in study of rhetoric, of philology, and of literature. Should be a study, not a pastime. Method of study must depend on point of view. Richard Grant White's dictum of reverent study. Dogmatism of commentators. Where Shakespeare's writings are to be found. Description of First Folio, by Richard Grant White. Rectification of errors. Different aspects of academic instruction in study of Shakespeare, of which the ethical is the highest

Method of study. Beware of too ambitious a design. Part better than the whole. Study from the historical standpoint; value of the Chronicle Plays ; value of the Roman Plays. Julius Cæsar, for educational purposes. First step ; to read it. How to pursue the study. The traveller's method of comprehending a city—Rome. Reconnaissance first, then critical study. Shakespeare and Plutarch. The sidelights and specific points of interest in Julius Cæsar. Each play must be studied with reference to its central idea. Illustrations of this canon. The Tragic Quadrilateral ; Lear, Othello, Macbeth and Hamlet. Natural movement and process of tragedy; from cause to crisis; thence, through its consequences, to the catastrophe. Illustration by triangle, or by Gervinus' arch. Shakespeare preserves our sense of moral proportion by adherence to this canon.............. **17**

LECTURE SECOND.

MACBETH.

Self-knowledge; its attainment under the light of intelligence and charity. The aid to be found in literature, the message of one man's genius to all men's hearts. The perennial sway of genius. Shakespeare, the supreme poet. His personality, his genius, his psychology. Macbeth, his greatest poem. Hallam's opinion; Drake's, Campbell's, Gervinus'. Its incompleteness in detail. An outline, or a torso? Swinburne's view. Shakespeare's great heroic drama. Its grandeur. Its problem obvious, but grand and pathetic. Hamlet and Macbeth, psychological complements; the vacillating will, the lawless will. Web of the plot; the story told. Felicity in selection of time, place, plot and theme of this tragedy; the time, a golden age; Scotland, a mysterious land; regicide, a timely and exciting theme; the problem, a contest for a human soul.

The Supernaturalism of Shakespeare. Popular beliefs as symbols of unseen forces. The first words of a play its keynote; illustrations. The Weird Sisters. Shakespeare's intuition of the loathsomeness of evil. The Weird Sisters real beings, tempters, mousing owls of Satan, but with no power over the conscience or will. Character of Macbeth at outset: lofty, valiant, energetic, imaginative, blunt, reticent, lawlessly ambitious. He entertains the temptation. His wife's part. Duncan's innocence. The *chiaro-oscuro* of murder. The action and reaction of murderous purpose. Character of Lady Macbeth. Shakespeare's absolute artistic perceptions in delineating characters illustrated. The feminine recoil in Lady Macbeth, and her remorse and death. Macbeth's indomitable energy and courage. The consequences of guilt;

CONTENTS.

the delusive promises of Satan; moral isolation. The lesson
of Macbeth: temptation, guilt, perdition. "Fear God and
keep His commandments." 41

LECTURE THIRD.

THE SIGNIFICANCE OF HAMLET.

The primacy in letters. Homer's place; Shakespeare's. The
Baconian paradox; its weakness. Comparison of Bacon's
actual gifts with Shakespeare's. Goethe's inspiration from
Shakespeare. Coleridge's estimate. A world literature
impossible to any writer. Shakespeare's true relations to
literature, and first place in it. Hamlet, his greatest creation. Comparison with his other plays. Its defects and
limitations but lays bare a human heart. Our debt to Goethe
for touching key-note of its meaning. Extracts from Wilhelm Meister discussing the play. Lecturer's modifications
of same. Werder's antagonistic interpretation. W. W.
Story's criticism of the German critics. Coleridge's interpretation; Lowell's. Manifold solutions of the play, especially by the Germans; Carl Karpf, Rœtschl, Freiligrath,
Sievers, Rohrbach, Benedix, Rapp, Voltaire, Chateaubriand.
Was Hamlet's madness real or feigned? Representation,
the province of the poet. Shakespeare's purpose in Hamlet
to portray a man, and the defeat of the human will. Hamlet
and Macbeth are complements, illustrating individual responsibility for our actions. How these questions are answered in each. Macbeth teaches the duty of rectitude of
will; Hamlet, of decision of will. Influence of Shakespeare's
germ of doubt on modern skepticism. Robert Elsmere.
Amiel's Journal. A Hamlet in real life. No escape from
the responsibility to act. The hesitation in the hero of Hamlet and the unexpectedness of the catastrophe necessary parts
of the tragic purpose. The lesson enforced, not in a type or
abstraction, but by portraying an individual man. Was it
himself? Kreyssig, Kenney, Hazlitt. "It is we who are Hamlet." "A No Philosopher;" the evolution of a human soul

in its totality presents a portrait. Hamlet's situation beyond *his* powers. His self-condemnation. Poetry is creation, not analysis. Each character a portrait, plus Shakespeare. Hamlet a likeness of the poet and of ourselves also—and of another. An image of the philosophic soul paralyzed by defect of will. The lesson of prompt and resolute action.... **12**

LECTURE FOURTH.

THE AUTHORSHIP OF HAMLET.

Their value my apology for extensive quotations in last lecture. Who wrote the original Hamlet? Three plays so named. The accepted version, or last Hamlet, based on Quarto Second, undoubtedly Shakespeare's. The First Quarto. Their titles. Their variance. Three theories to account for the intrinsic character of Q 1; 1st, A mangled copy of Q 2; 2nd, Clarendon Editors', partly Shakespeare's based on an older play by another hand; 3rd, an older form of play, but Shakespeare's own. When Q 2 was written. Footnote on the Inhibition. Title-pages of the two Quartos express their real difference. How Q 1 came to be printed. Q 2 an evolution from Q 1. Q 1 probably an actor's copy used at the Universities, but essentially Shakespearian. The First Hamlet a hypothetical play, not extant; probably differing somewhat from Q 1. This original draft generally assumed not to be by Shakespeare. Burden of proof on those who deny his authorship. Halliwell takes alien authorship for granted. Review of evidence. Clarendon Editors believe it unworthy of Shakespeare in 1589. Who was adequate to the task? Fleay's conjecture of Marlowe's joint authorship. Most opponents of Shakespeare's authorship argue from his want of ability or preparation at that time. These arguments and the Clarendon theory mutually destructive. The youthful Shakespeare not equal to his later self, but superior to all others. Probable date of composition of First Hamlet in 1587. C. A. Brown's opinion of its authorship. View of Knight and others. Value of opinion of Clarendon Editors.

CONTENTS.

Francis Meres' list of plays considered. His opinion of Shakespeare. Incorrect inference from his List. Temporary eclipse of Hamlet in 1596, and reasons for its final revision then. Malone's theory of Kyd's authorship. His incongruous and untenable grounds. Skottowe, Collier, Dyce, Fleay, Symonds, on this point. "The play within a play" as evidence. Other instances of same. No evidence at all of Kyd's authorship, and Marlowe's share a mere surmise. Shakespeare alone equal to it. Shakespeare's, the only tragedies that survive. Two bands of literary wreckers at work on Shakespeare. Elze's argument from Euphuism, of an early production of Hamlet; also of its evolution from Hamnet's birth and death. Nash's allusion in 1589. Fleay's belief controverted that this refers to Shakespeare as an actor only. "The Noverint." Greene's "Shakescene" in 1592. Chettle's apology. Henslow's Diary says Hamlet was acted in 1594. Lodge's reference in 1596. Summing up of the evidence. The positive evidence all in favor of Shakespeare's authorship. Flimsy character of the negative evidence. Shakespeare's genius phenomenal, but not abnormal. His long continued and undisputed title to this play and his transcendent genius sufficient grounds for our belief. Incorrect notions of genius. Its elements. Shakespeare's conformity to its criteria. The author of First Hamlet........ 105

LECTURE FIFTH.

THE EVOLUTION OF HAMLET.

Shakespeare, the founder of the romantic drama. The other dramatists, his successors and disciples. The exception, the University Group. Fleay' surmise of collaboration with Marlowe. Comment. Marlowe's ability. Baselessness of the conjectural criticism that assigns Shakespeare's plays to other writers. His competitors were contemporaries rather than predecessors. Lyly and Peele ; Marlowe. Argument based on Shakespeare's intellectual sterility, irrational; that on his youth, equally so. Marlowe's case. Undisputed contemporary opinion the only proof of authorship by any of the dramatists of that day. Their personal obscurity. Shakespeare's education. Ben Jonson's estimate of him. His small indebtedness to others. His theatrical career. Venus and Adonis. His ability to write the original Hamlet. Other instances of equally precocious genius. Objections to Shakespeare's ability ever to have written his plays. Smith's "Bacon and Shakespeare." Theory of his nonentity considered. Was he a lawyer's clerk? Lord Campbell's book; Cartwright's. Inferences from his legal phraseology in Hamlet. Public disregard of dramatic authors. Hartley Coleridge's favorable deductions from the absence of proof of evil against them. Shakespeare's worth as a man. Little known of personality of writers even now. Contemporary opinion of Shakespeare; Ben Jonson, Meres, Weever, Sir John Davies' verses. Shakespeare's call to the stage and his rapid rise. His dramatic method and creative faculty. The co-operative mode of producing plays; their plots. Growth of Hamlet. Revision in 1596. Reasons for it. Its pessimism. W. W. Story's criticism. The personality in Hamlet. Hamlet's death. Shakespeare's dream and waking. Possible disappointment in friendship. The dregs of sin. Entry in Stationer's Register in 1602. Erroneous inferences. The Last Hamlet saturated with Shakespeare's personality. Hamlet, an evolution. The particular portrait becomes the mirror of all mankind.................................. 134

LECTURE SIXTH.

THE PLOT OF HAMLET.

Toleration and fanaticism in critical literature. The full and final significance of Hamlet not contained in first draft. The highest ideals often originate in the least ambitious designs. How Shakespeare came to create Hamlet; the times, the

CONTENTS. 13

environment, the antecedents. The spirit of the age. Elizabethan England, an era of awakening, action and questioning. The demand for truth. The intense nationality and patriotism of Englishmen and of Shakespeare. His reverent skepticism. His purpose in writing this play. Shakespeare a poet, but also a courtier, a play-writer and a patriot. Political uses of the drama

The political situation in 1586. Covert war. Elizabeth and Mary Stuart. Public demand for death of latter. All of Shakespeare's patrons among her enemies. Her execution determined on. Attitude and character of James VI of Scotland. The Master of Gray's letter. King James to be appeased. All means tried. The play as a political device; instances. Loyal rage against Mary. Her death. Elizabeth's tortuous repudiation of it and peril to her Council. Justification needed. The rebuke of regicide and of vacillation illustrated in Hamlet. Probability of Shakespeare's employment. Dramatic fecundity of the day. The plot of Hamlet fits the case of the murder of Darnley. A pattern for it twenty years old. Sir Wm. Drury's Letter. Prototypes of the persons of the drama. My adoption of this theory. Rev. Mr. Plumptre's pamphlet in 1796. Furness' summary of it. Resemblances of plot of Hamlet to the murder of Darnley. Likeness of Hamlet to King James in character. Silberschlag's support of same theory. Comments of Moberly and Hunter. Confirmation of arguments by discovery of Q 1 in 1823. Grounds for this theory are: 1st, the motives of British Government for employing this device; 2nd, resemblance of plot and details to death of Darnley, and similarity of character of Hamlet and James. Where and what is Shakespeare's Denmark. Its identity with Scotland, illustrated by geography, customs and personal traits of the characters. Lowell's comment on the condition of social transition in Hamlet. Scotland exactly answers it. James VI's personal legacy of revenge. His vacillating and equivocal nature and policy. Hamlet's self-reproach for hesitation in revenge. Suggestions of the play to the King.. 160

LECTURE SEVENTH.

THE PROTOTYPE OF HAMLET.

Origin of plot. Saxo-Grammaticus. Belleforest's version. The English translation. Unlikeness to the play. Its date. Contrasts. Comparison of legend and the play. The brief widowhood of Mary Stuart and Gertrude. Their marriage with the murderers. The physical beauty of The Ghost and of Darnley, and the ugliness of Bothwell and Claudius. The tenure of the royal title. The title of Claudius as King Consort, legal. Note on "imperial jointress." Succession by bequest. Hamlet's claim. Dilemma of Hamlet. His irresolution. Revenge for regicide taught him as a duty. The penalty of a refusal of responsibility. The "Blood-Tragedy," "Hamlet, Revenge!", a stepping-stone to Shakespeare's promotion. The son of murdered Darnley naturally the prototype of the son of murdered Denmark. Identity in character. Sir Antony Weldon's sketch of James. Scott's, in "The Fortunes of Nigel." The Venetian Ambassador's sketch. Bishop Hacket's. Comparison of James with these accounts. To Shakespeare and English loyalists— the Coming Man, the Prince! Hamlet fits into this character. Is the creation of an ideal organic man in fiction possible without an actual archetype in real life? Only mortals become immortal, like Hamlet. Portraiture is representation of an organism as viewed in the mind of the artist. An ideal is an image with something of the artist put into it. Hamlet, at first altogether James, was evolved, by Shakespeare putting himself into it. A Kentucky theory of Hamlet as "a scoundrel." His brutality to Ophelia; his projects, plots, indirections, quibblings, and cowardice. Contrasts in James and Hamlet accounted for......................

Argument based on Hamlet's age. The same as James'. Thirty years old in 1596. Proofs. Only twenty when play first written in 1586. Proofs. Supposed inconsistency between first part of play and last due to the Revision. Furnivall; Halliwell's unauthorized sacrifice of the text. Perennial youth of fictitious characters. Real people grow older.

Hamlet grew older. "Full forty years" changed to "Full thirty years," in the Revision. Goethe's portraiture of Polonius; of Rosencrantz and Guildenstern. Bothwell's Confession. "The beauteous majesty of Denmark." Froude's Mary Stuart. Swinburne's apostrophe to her. Who was Fortinbras? Summing up of the evidence. The body of Hamlet is James; the Divinity that animates him, Shakespeare 192

PREFACE.

THE lectures contained in this volume were prepared for the senior classes in Tulane College and in the H. Sophie Newcomb Memorial College for young women. But, in deference to a wish expressed by many lovers of literature, they were included in the courses of free public lectures on literature and science, delivered each year in Tulane University to the people of New Orleans. Having proved acceptable to large and intelligent audiences, they are now submitted to other students who take an interest in the subject, with the hope that they may add something in the way of suggestion to a reverent and intelligent study of the great dramatist.

The author has adhered to the form of lectures in which the subject was originally presented, since it was the spontaneous cast of his thought, and probably contains "more matter with less art" than if he should attempt to conform it to a more regular model.

In his interpretation of Shakespeare, truth, not novelty, has been the writer's aim; and this, he believes, is to be found in the broad lines laid down by the giants of philosophical criticism, rather than in the iridescence of paradox, as illustrated in lesser lights.

The chief problem and main contention in these papers is, however, for a proposition that may strike the reader as probable, plausible, or possibly preposterous, according to his point of view. The theory is maintained that, in his original conception of Hamlet, Shakespeare found the prototype of the Prince in James VI. of Scotland, and that the plot was greatly influenced by political events arising out of the murder of Darnley and the execution of Mary, Queen of Scots. The hypothesis is not altogether novel, but the present writer arrived at it by independent study, and has maintained it by facts unknown to the first propounder. Whether convincing or not, it is thought that the theory is founded on sound induction, and will, at least, prove curiously suggestive. If the readers of this book receive from it a small proportion of the pleasure the writer has felt in consulting the sources from which it is derived, he will be amply repaid; and his object will be wholly attained if these lectures shall be accepted among the judicious as in any wise a valuable contribution to that body of Shakespearean study which is doing so much to stimulate and elevate the thought of our race.

WM. PRESTON JOHNSTON.

TULANE UNIVERSITY,
NEW ORLEANS, La, *April*, 1890.

THE PROTOTYPE OF HAMLET

AND

OTHER SHAKESPEARIAN PROBLEMS.

HOW TO STUDY SHAKESPEARE.

"What is the end of study? let me know."
Love's Labor's Lost, *1*, *1*.

It is a matter of general remark that, in the last few years, literature has become fashionable in New Orleans. This means more than at first sight appears. It means that our people, and especially our women, have set for themselves a higher ideal than the old-time dance and piano; and I say this without the slightest disrespect for these or any other legitimate forms of recreation. The feeling has come home to our best and strongest women, those who mould and sway the opinions of the mass, that they must not delay to enter into that higher realm of thought which lifts humanity, even so much as one step, nearer to the Divine Archetype. And they have judged aright when they decided that this was to be found in the best literature. For the best literature embodies the best thought of the highest thnkers, addressed to the hearts of all mankind. That true literature is the mother of culture, none will gainsay who have nursed at her breast. Literature, to be true, must be holy, catholic, apostolic. It is one form of the Church of God, one medium by which the Divine spirit, through human means, reveals the divine truth to human hearts. It is not true literature unless it is holy, holy in every sense, healthgiving and inspiring to the moral nature; catholic, addressed to all hearts, to our common humanity; apostolic, the divine message, the truth once delivered to the saints, the gospel or word of God carried forth to the world by those who are heaven-chosen to that end. Let me say, once for all, that any specious form of falsehood or *diablerie*, any ministration to the baser nature of man, is neither true art nor true literature. It is sham and veneering that will blister and peel and go to pieces under any honest heat of discussion. That an aspiration for true literature exists to-day in New Orleans is, therefore, certainly a most encouraging feature of our society. The question is how this University may contribute somewhat towards gratifying so generous an impulse.

To this end we have had the honor this year, through the kindness of Professors Ficklen and Fortier, to open up to you a view of the early dramatic literature of England and France, the beginnings of the Drama; for, strangely enough, under the much mixed morality of the Drama, its masquerading and its rough and robust wrestling with truth, we often perceive the ethical problem more clearly than when formulated as sententious morality. It is in no

spirit of depreciation or disparagement of other forms
of literature, however, that we invite you to some
studies in the drama, pointing out a pathway for
your footsteps rather than attempting to garner for
you its full sheaves. History and fiction are of the
utmost importance for both training and inspiration,
and may evoke the highest powers of mind and
soul. Poetry warms the heart, kindles the intellect,
and exalts the imagination. But in no other department of literature is the implicit moral culture which
reveals character-growth more effective than in the
Drama.

When we speak of the Drama the mind naturally
reverts to the plays of Shakespeare. Next to the
Bible they have the strongest hold on the thought
of the civilized world. Without inquiring here into
the cause, such is undoubtedly the fact. They furnish an inexhaustible field for the ingenuity of the
commentator, whether his criticism touches on the
archæology, the philology, or the philosophy, contained in the text. In them the psychologist realizes
the evolution of human character in its artistic completeness, under the pressure of moral circumstances
and of temptation, while the great, uncritical public
consumes edition after edition of his works, and
notes, essays, and commentaries innumerable, with
as real a sense of gratification. The rude boards of
the provincial theatre and the great temples of dramatic art alike resound to the utterances of the bard,
century after century, while boasted rivals seem but
an ephemeral and flitting fashion, to-day in vogue,
to-morrow forgotten. The popularity of Shakespeare

is apparently limitless and growing ; and if, sometimes, it exhibits the absurdities and erratic motions that deform every cultus and every form of hero-worship, yet we cannot disbelieve that it rests upon a real foundation, and that a solid substratum, a true bed-rock of genius, underlies the masterpieces of the prince of dramatists. One great advantage to be derived from the selection of Shakespeare as a study by those who are entering upon the pursuits of literature is that his works are deeply interesting ; and it is hard to over-estimate the importance of a genuine interest in the subject of any study. It means present vigilant attention, vivid apprehension, clear and complete conceptions, fresh and enduring recollection. It means business. It means mastery. It means appropriation, use, ownership, of a subject.

But these plays are not merely current coin ; they are thought-breeders. They arouse the dormant or sluggish imagination. They people the mind, not with lay figures, but with living beings, who cry out continually to the heart and soul, "Awake; beware." They present the problems of existence, not in formulas, but in concrete men and women, saying, doing, and thinking, as we say, do, and think, and subjected to the immutable law of moral cause and consequence. Hence Shakespeare's plays are a philosophy more profound than the Dialogues of Plato and the Socratic discussions, in that they are exactly conformed to nature.

If the literary models of Greece and Rome are the sole standards of art, the dramas of Shakespeare are not art, because they vary from these standards.

But if a Gothic cathedral embodies art, though in forms infinitely more complex, as truly as the Parthenon, then Hamlet, as well as Antigone, is art. If the landscapes of Church, or the drawings of Doré, are legitimate expressions of our æsthetic nature as surely as bas-reliefs from Athens or Olympia, then the Merchant of Venice and the Tempest are as true to fundamental art canons as the Iliad, the Aecestis, or the Birds. Shakespeare's creative genius constituted a new cycle of art, the cycle of nature as distinguished from that of conventional form; and what can be more inspiring than to receive the key to a new realm of art?

Shakespeare, next to the Bible, is the best manual in which to study rhetoric; and for the simple reason that rhetoric is the science and art of most effectively expressing thought in language, and in Shakespeare the language does not merely clothe the thought, but actually embodies it. His "beauties," as they are called, admirable thoughts couched in words of exquisite fitness, have entered into the proverbial philosophy of the British race; it may be said, indeed, into the body of aphoristic wisdom of the whole world. The sayings of the persons of his drama have crystallized into gems of thought, and longer passages linger, like familiar strains, in aged and weary memories.

These works afford opportunity for the least irksome form of philological study. When language study is pursued by the historical method, backward or forward, we find in the sunburst of the Shakespearean drama its most vivid and imaginative form, and a phase absolutely necessary to a complete comprehension of the genius of the English tongue.

Many will be found to agree with me that for a serious study of English literature, whoever else may be named as second, Shakespeare must be placed first. He is to us what Homer was to the Greeks. I may say, though with diffidence, he is more. He is our teacher, master, educator, in that prime philosophy, a knowledge of the human heart. Should we not make his works, then, a study rather than a pastime? If it be wise to sit where the chance drops of his world-wisdom may fall upon and bedew our robes, were it not better to go forth like him who walks in an April shower, when spring scatters her jewels with prodigal hand, till all our garments are moist and saturate with the descending floods? Is it not better to be the disciple of the largest and most liberal sage in all our literature than to speak in the words of any other master?

But let us suppose it admitted that Shakespeare is the most, or at least a most, desirable study for the lover of literature, how are we to get the best results from such study? The method to be adopted must of course depend largely on the end in view, and will vary with the age, attainment, experience, and tastes of the student; and it must also depend largely, of course, upon the special culture of the teacher, and the standpoint from which he approaches his subject. But it may be laid down as a fundamental canon in the study of literature that it must be pursued in the literature itself, and not in what is said about it. That fierce Shakespearian, Richard Grant White, says of his book, "Shakespeare's Scholar:" "It attempts not to decide what Shakespeare might have written or what he could have written, or to seek the interpretation of his thoughts from those who proclaim themselves his prophets, but to learn from him what he did write, and to study to understand *that* in the submissive yet still inquiring spirit with which a neophyte listens to the teachings of a revered and no less beloved master." And then he goes on to castigate "the editors, commentators, and verbal critics," rejoicing that he has "kept free from the contamination and perversion of their instruction."

While Mr. White was undoubtedly correct in his main idea, and a very good understanding may be had of the current of Shakespeare's thought by reverent and unaided study of his text, few readers will be found to agree with him, when he says, "It is folly to say that the writings of such a man need notes and comments to enable readers of ordinary intelligence to apprehend their full meaning." It all depends on what the notes are. The methods pursued by the commentators of the last century, the egotistic and elephantine dogmatism of Warburton and Johnson and the wild guesses of many others, are enough to provoke a more saint-like temper than Mr. White's. They are well parodied by that critic who said, "Shakespeare could not have written:

> 'Sermons in stones, books in the running brooks,
> And good in everything:'

that was nonsense. He must have written: 'Sermons in books, stones in the running brooks;' those were *facts* that could be proved."

"A reverent study," as White says, will, however, accomplish much. Indeed, this is the main thing; study, not skirmishing. Many, I trust, will be found in this audience willing to devote their time to this study, and it will be the object of this lecture, without attempting at all to exhaust the subject, to furnish a few hints that may prove useful to such as are in earnest in the matter. And I may say here that I feel all the real difficulties involved in my present attempt, which must presuppose in my audience an interest already established in the topic; and I must rely for success more upon the instruction conveyed than upon the amusement that is generally looked for in the lecture-hall.

Having determined to study Shakespeare, the first step to be taken is to discover where his writings are to be found, as he wrote them. After almost three hundred years of shifting and change—of process—the text has nearly, though not quite, settled down to a standard, which may, or may not, be what the poet wrote. This standard, more fluctuating than a bi-metallic one, sways gently to and fro between Knight and White and Wright, and Hudson and Halliwell and Hazlitt, and many, many more, of whom each reader may take his choice. As a rule, I am content with the admirable Clarendon edition of Shakespeare's Plays, though Furness furnishes us with a variety of versions in his Variorum editions, so that a captious critic can pursue therein the round of Shakespearian study with a go-as-you-please gait. Scientific criticism has, in the crucible of common-sense, reduced much of the crude ore of eighteenth century commentary, and given us genuine metal in its stead as the result. But the youthful student may well ask: "Why was all this necessary? Why not give us just what Shakespeare wrote?" That is exactly what the labor of a hundred commentators means. But again it will be inquired: "Why all their toil?" And the reply is, "To arrive at what he actually did write."

It is familiar, of course, to Shakespearian scholars that the Plays of Shakespeare were not printed until 1623, seven years after his death, and then in the form known as the First Folio, which, though evidently full of flagrant errors, "is the only admitted authority for the text of his dramatic works." The First Folio contemned previous editions, as "stolen and surreptitious copies, maimed and deformed by the frauds and stealths of injurious impostors," and aimed to give a true copy of Shakespeare's plays; but that enthusiastic student of Shakespeare, Richard Grant White, scarcely overestimates the defects of the First Folio itself in the following animated description of it. "Such is the authority of this First Folio, that had it been printed with ordinary care, there would have been no appeal from its text; and editorial labors in the publication of Shakespeare's works, except from such as might think it necessary and proper to obtrude explanatory notes and critical comments upon his readers, would have been not only without justification but without opportunity. But, unfortunately, this precious folio is one of the worst printed books that ever issued from the press. It is filled with the grossest possible errors in orthography, punctuation, and arrangement. It is not surprising that Mr. Collier estimates the corrections of 'minor errors'—that is, of mere palpable misspelling and mispunctuation—in his amended folio, at twenty thousand. The first folio must contain quite as many such blunders; and the second is worse in this respect than the first. But, beside minor errors, the correction of which is obvious, words are so transformed as to be past recognition, even with the aid of the context; lines are transposed; sentences are sometimes broken by a full point followed by a capital letter, and other times have their members displaced and mingled in incomprehensible confusion; verse printed as prose, and prose as verse; speeches belonging to one character are given to another; and, in brief, all the possible varieties of typographical derangement abound in that volume, in the careful printing of which of all others, save one, the world was most interested. This it is which has made the labors of careful and learned editors necessary for the text of Shakespeare; and which has furnished the excuse for the exhibition of more pedantry, foolishness, conceit, and presumption than have been exhibited upon any other subject—always except that of religion."

In the rectification of these errors, the commentators have gone back to earlier editions of single plays for comparison, and to conjectural emendations based upon common sense, uncommon sense, and often upon nonsense. Every resource of antiquarian zeal, philological training, and contemporaneous illustration has been invoked to redeem the text from its imperfections. That the result has not been fully attained as yet is only to say that human nature is fallible; but we have to-day practically a far better expression of the poet's thought than could probably have been heard on any stage, and certainly than could have been read in any book or manuscript, existing in his lifetime, or until the present time.

In academic instruction a much greater share is given to philological training, to the linguistics of the author, than would be practicable or profitable under other circumstances; and even here it is often carried, as I have sometimes felt in my own teaching of college classes, further than is wise. For, however valuable verbal discipline may be to the scholar, it is very easy to sacrifice to it more important considerations. The æsthetic value of the author and the artistic form of his work have a higher claim upon the attention of the student, while the psychological side of his dramatic personages and the evolution of character by touches which are consummate, because the perfection of the natural method in art and literature, demand our closest attention. Last and best, perhaps, is the ethical aspect, in which, viewing a play as an organic unit, we grasp its ethical content, that implicit moral problem which, though not visibly exposed to the eye, strikes the mind and rings the tocsin of the heart and conscience like a fire alarm. Let us see how, taking up the study of Shakespeare's Plays, we may get at as much of all this as is possible under ordinarily favorable circumstances.

In the first place, I should say, do not begin with

too wide a plan, unless everything concurs to forward your design. Recollect that an encyclopædia, useful as it is for reference, is the worst text-book and the worst literature in the world, and that you get less of real history in a universal history than, I might say, in the biography of one great man— Cæsar, or Cromwell, or Bonaparte, or Washington. If the student chance to be an ardent lover of that grand segment of English history which began with Runnymede and the Magna Charta, and closed with the Reformation, the Renaissance, and the Rise of Democratic Thought, he may select for his study Shakespeare's magnificent cycle of historical dramas, and even supplement them with the Chronicle plays of his contemporaries, which fill the gaps he has left. In these can be traced English history from King John to Henry VIII., embodied in a stirring form of English literature ; and, if backed, verified, and corrected by a reasonable knowledge of the annals of the times, it will present to the mind a most vivid picture of the age of chivalry. The series is, in fact, though not in form, a grand trilogy, in which liberty lifts itself, like the rainbow's arch, from its rugged base of feudal privilege under the Plantagenets to its splendid culmination in the conquest of France, and then declines to the catastrophe of despotism under the Tudors. In the blended colors of historic circumstance, personal intervention, and race-characteristics, we may trace the unerring curve of cause and consequence, and behold the national progress bridging with airy span the mental horizon, like a structure of the Gods set on high by the hand of destiny. This is a noble and suggestive course of study for the lover of history. I do not say it is the best, for the Roman Plays, Coriolanus, Julius Cæsar, and Antony and Cleopatra afford an equal field of research and comparative historical study, and in a finer form of literature than the English Chronicle Plays. Indeed, there is no single play which has been more generally used for educational purposes than Julius Cæsar. While by no means the loftiest or most perfect type of Shakespeare's tragedy, it contains so many excellences that it is well fitted for a text-book in this department of study. Craik's "English of Shakespeare," Abbott's Shakespearian Grammar, Rolfe's, or the Clarendon, edition of the play, and numerous commentaries can be drawn into aids in this study.

Suppose now we select Julius Cæsar as our opening study, what is the first step to be taken? To read it. Simple as this rule appears, it is not always followed; and the professor or lecturer often engages in the discussion of a play, known to his listeners only after the vaguest fashion. It is best for the learner to read it in his own way, at home, getting what he can out of it without too much effort, and laying hold on what most interests him individually. Then, when he comes to the audience chamber, the teacher can take him from one point of view to another, until the whole tragedy gathers form and rises before his vision like some fair city as seen from its acropolis.

To the traveller who for the first time visits Rome

the natural impulse must arise at once to ascend the Capitol, or St. Peter's dome, and with a sweep of the eye to take in the panorama of the ages, as marked out in the mouldering monuments at his feet. The mingled mass of ruins, relics, and recent structures would convey in some half-intelligible way a conception of the greatness and decay, the vicissitudes and vitality, of the Eternal City. Gradually his heart would become attuned to the key-note of fallen glory, to whose rhythm its history for fifteen centuries has been set; and as his ear caught the far-off strains of imperial sway, and the still more distant martial usic of republican masterhood, the whole orchestra of the past would burst upon his soul. Descending to its streets, he would stand in the Forum, traverse the ancient ways, gaze upon deserted temples, arches of triumph, and a shattered Colosseum, until the deeds of kings, consuls, emperors, and popes, and the words of poets, orators, historians, and philosophers, rose to his memory and grouped themselves into a perpetual pageant. Let him once again mount to his coign of vantage, and look down upon the maze below. With what an unsealed vision will he now survey the scene. An old, and an older, Rome rise before him like exhalations, and he sees each, concrete, definite, entire. Rome lives again. The analogy to the scholar who first approaches some masterpiece of literature with reverential eye is too close and too obvious to be disregarded. He first surveys, then studies in its details, and then groups into one broad, distinct, and powerful conception the entire work. It is thus that a drama of Shakespeare may be mastered and brought within our intellectual dominion.

Hence it seems judicious first to read the play as a whole, taking in as much of it as the mind's eye can readily cover and understand with its unaided power. This reconnaissance made, we come down to our maps, and compare them critically with the topography and all its landmarks; that is to say, we go to the sources of historical information from which Shakespeare wove the plot and evolved the drama, say, of Julius Cæsar. These we find in the pages of Plutarch; and cold, indeed, must be the imagination of the youth which does not kindle under the inspiration of the old Greek biographer and moralist. Yet in reading the Julius Cæsar of Shakespeare and the lives of the Romans by Plutarch, one cannot but be struck with the immense difference between a man of first-rate talents and a man of genius; though it would be fairer to say, between Shakespeare and any other writer. A portraiture by Plutarch stands like the Parthenon, a perfect building, in the cold gray of dawn; but, when the sunlight of Shakespeare's creative force falls upon its front, from the Acropolis which serves as its pedestal to its very summit it glows with the divine splendor of intellectual illumination.

Still, Plutarch's Lives cannot be called history, according to our modern philosophical and scientific conception of history, as actual fact permeated with essential truth. They are moral ideals illustrated by legendary pictures. If the purpose of the teacher embraces in its scope historical instruction, as has generally been my own case, he may properly require some reading of the events of the Julian period from such manual as may be preferred, and, if possible, a rapid study of Froude's vivid biography of "the foremost man of all this world." Further, it will certainly be a great gain if the teacher can, during these studies, point out how nearly each author conforms to actual fact and how nearly to ideal verity, and, noting their discrepancies, invite inquiry and discussion of whatever questions may arise, great and small, whether it be the true characters of the arch-conspirators, or even the names, spelling, and birthplaces of the more obscure. And here it may be added that this is not so much for the value of the facts themselves, as for their use as pegs to hang thoughts upon, links in the mnemotechnic chain which binds together the whole body of the argument.

It may properly be asked whether this method does not really violate the grand canon laid down in the beginning of this essay, that literature should be taught in literature, and not in what is said about it. There is danger of this, and it must be avoided. The excursions should be rapid and not too wide. But still, to see any object distinctly, to comprehend it fully, we must not be content with a glance or even a single view of it; we must see it under every light and shadow, and from every point of view. And if we make our prime study of the play of Julius Cæsar historical, it is because the author himself conceives it as real history, though under somewhat crude forms. On the other hand, in the study of other plays, such as the Tempest or As You Like It, the historical element may be very summarily dealt with, or even entirely neglected.

Now, when we again take up the play, it is no longer a play; it is a life. And it is not a screed about a life, but a live life being lived; people planning, plotting, striving, quarrelling, killing, and dying greatly and nobly. As then we proceed to review the drama, scene by scene and act by act, the question continually arises, what bearing has this word, or passage, or rendering on the theories, political, ethical, or psychological, which have been engaging our attention. Comment, suggestion, and inquiry should invite the student to the contemplation and solution of these. Was Cæsar's usurpation necessary or justifiable? Was his genius for destruction or for organization? By what casuistry do the champions of *de jure* and *de facto* governments vindicate the protagonists of the Roman Commonwealth? Was Cæsar rightfully slain? Should Brutus have died as he did? What was Cæsar's apparition? But it is not necessary to multiply these questions. They will occur to each one according to his mental constitution or education. Their consideration and solution set the student thinking, and develop the power to originate and discuss, which is one grand object of literary culture.

By this time each student has his theory, right or wrong, of the whole play. In working out the details, the language has become familiar by repeated reference. Unconsciously almost, the reader has caught the spirit of the play, and the words which embody it rise naturally to his lips. But they rise, not with parrot-like iteration, but as the expression of kindling thought. The time has now arrived for the student to formulate his views in well-considered essays, and to become familiar with the beauty, force, and fitness of the more splendid or significant passages, sounding their depths, and plucking out the very heart of their mystery.

During the whole of the aforementioned course of instruction the philological value of particular words, and their history and use, may be brought under discussion. With such a text-book in hand as Craik's English of Shakespeare, the danger is of doing too much rather than too little of this sort of work. To allure the student into paths of English philology, not to exact from him a formal task therein, but still more to elucidate the text, should be the teacher's object. Hence, these investigations should be incidental, and not as the goal of steady effort.

It is not too much to say that a body of students will rise from a study of Julius Cæsar according to the method I have sketched, not only enlightened by valuable information and fuller knowledge of how to obtain it, but with a larger view of the value of literature itself and keener appetite for its pursuits; in a word, liberalized, set free from that thraldom to the letter which kills high thought, and with their feet set in the right path toward a true culture.

I might here pause, as the foregoing illustrates one method of studying Shakespeare, which has greatly commended itself to me. But it may be well to remark that each play must be studied with reference to its centre of interest, and with a treatment varying according to its central idea. Guided by this canon, the reader, if his taste or fancy attracts him to the comedy rather than the tragedy of Shakespeare, will find therein a wonderfully wide range of character, incident, and eloquent or witty speech, and always, too, a central or dominant idea that will repay his search. The Merchant of Venice oscillates between extremes, from the tender dalliance of moonlit lovers to the perilous verge of intensest tragic motive, while, in elaborating its plan of construction, Gervinus traces through the tangle of its plots a design arabesque in its intricacy. As You Like It has been made familiar to lovers of the stage by many charming actresses, and the melancholy Jaques, with his pessimistic meditations, is better known than any actual gentleman of his day. And under the airy movement and poetic conception of the Tempest is veiled a very mine of spiritual force, as the summer cloud is charged with the electric bolt.

Still guided by this canon, we may, for instance, take up that superb Quadrilateral of Tragedy, whose grim bastions frown down upon all adventure that would scale their impregnable ramparts; for Lear, Othello, Macbeth, and Hamlet still stand as the very citadel of Shakespeare's fame. In these, as in most of Shakespeare's tragedies, we may discover the normal evolution of the plot, as pointed out by Gervinus, and which must have been suggested by an unerring instinct of genius to Shakespeare. The natural movement and process of tragedy is from cause to crisis, and from crisis to catastrophe. A triangle, or perhaps an arch, as suggested by Gervinus, will fairly present the development of the tragic process from cause to catastrophe.

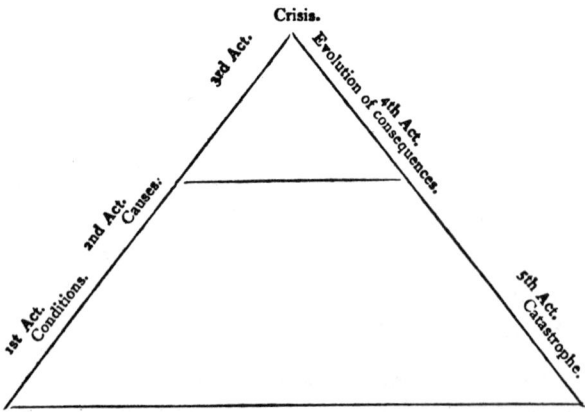

The first two acts should exhibit the moral and intellectual conflict between opposing motives, which ought naturally to culminate near the middle of the third act, or centre of a play, in a decisive deed, the consequences of which should, in the latter half of the tragedy, show its necessary effect in the final catastrophe. The opening scenes display the persons of the drama, and lay down the conditions of the plot. The controlling motive should there develop itself, leading the protagonist, or hero, to that event which constitutes the crisis of the action, and which, under the decision of his free-will, becomes a destiny to him. He has by his own deeds made a bed, and must lie in it. He has dug a pit, and he will fall into it. He has set toils, and he cannot escape from them. As a chief interest in the causative, or early, half of the tragedy is in observing the oscillation of the balance, the scruple that decides the tempted man in making choice of his course, so in the last two acts we are aroused to a still keener curiosity, and perhaps sympathy, in watching his struggle to escape from the consequences of his act, or in witnessing the silent and inevitable steps by which, guiding his descent to the catastrophe, Nemesis exacts her penalty, through expiation or destruction.

In a drama thus constructed, the attention is kept aroused, the sense of symmetry is satisfied by a just balance of the parts, and the moral lesson which is the ultimate purpose of the tragedy is duly and clearly enforced. Shakespeare, with all his alleged disregard for form, preserves, as a rule, the sense of moral proportion in his plays by an adherence to this canon of dramatic construction, constituting, as it does, the fundamental and only genuine unity in the playwright's art.

In Macbeth and Hamlet the historical and mythical element admit and require some discussion, but the main interest centres on their psychology, and this has been illustrated by so many hands as to demand here a mere allusion. The reaction of motive and deed upon character, resulting in consequences which form the staple of the drama, will, in these tragedies, employ the powers of instructor and disciple in the work of analysis, and finally in that supreme effort of reconstruction which beholds the spiritual image that is mirrored in the incidents of the play, and evolves its moral purpose from shadowy belongings.

The artistic beauty and wonderful imagery of these tragedies are brought out in their full force while following the clue of character woven into their royal drapery; and tangled and perhaps insoluble mysteries of human destiny are proposed, which test and measurably baffle our curiosity and subtle questioning.

In the short course of lectures which I purpose to give, it is possible to approach the study of the Shakespearian drama from only one or two sides. If broader aspects of the theme are desired, as they certainly are most desirable, they are at hand in the most alluring form, and can be found in the essays of Hudson, Whipple, Lowell, Richard Grant White, Charles Knight, and many others.

The lectures following will be confined to a single one on Macbeth, in which its ethical aspects are more particularly treated, and five lectures on Hamlet, which I hope may not prove unacceptable to the lovers of the nobler forms of the drama. If they shall stimulate thought, invite inquiry, and lead to a more correct appreciation of our greatest poet, their object will have been answered.

Personally, I am amply rewarded if I can in the least do my part to stir the teeming literary aspiration of New Orleans to a calm and loving survey of the higher walks of literature.

MACBETH.

> "Thriftless ambition that will ravin up
> Thine own life's means."
> *Macbeth*, II., 4.

KNOW thyself. Such is the mandate of the best Greek philosophy, and such the mandate of the last scientific criticism. We all desire knowledge, and this self-knowledge especially invites our inquiry. But there is no algebra of the understanding which has formulated the spiritual nature in abstract terms. Our only really valuable knowledge of the immaterial spirit comes to us in a different way. It breaks upon us, as we get out of the darkness into the light, by looking steadily at man—at his spiritual essence, as it is manifested all about us, in the meanest as well as in the greatest. And we grasp this knowledge in its fulness by looking at this poor human soul, not under the glare of artificial lights, but in the softened glow of God's own sunshine, under the chastening influence of that sweet charity which is the divinest of our faculties. This light of intelligence, and this sweetness of charity together constitute that culture which sums up modern philosophic education.

It is not for all of us, or any of us, to walk in the

full light of the meridian sun ; perhaps it is not best for us so to do ; but still we must seek for light everywhere. One of our best aids in this acquisition of self-knowledge, this clear conception of the human soul, is found in literature. I mean by literature the message of one man's genius to all men's hearts. The great masters, the leaders of thought, the princes and pontiffs of poesy and philosophy, the bards and sages, have each their message, fire-winged and voiceful, which summons its circle of disciples, and creates its school or sect. Take Homer, and now, twenty-five centuries having passed, we see Great Britain's Prime Ministers, Gladstone, master of finance, leaving his budget to explain the intricacies of Homeric thought, and Derby, the sturdy statesman, translating the resounding lines of the Iliad into English verse ; and Pope and Cowper, and Lang, and our American Bryant, and a hundred more, each making his own version of the father of song. Think how Aristotle has swayed the minds of age after age of reasoners, and how Plato still asserts a claim to dominion wherever philosophy lifts her eyes to the stars. But I may not dwell too long on this quickening power of literature, with its divine messages to the human race, lest I be drawn aside from the special subject of this essay.

When we look abroad through the wide provinces of literature for a man to whom all concede that divine insight into the human soul which is the real definition of genius, and from whose words we may catch its inspiration, and obtain that self-knowledge which is literature's highest function, common acclaim, the voice of the many and the voice of the mighty, accords a supreme excellence to Shakespeare. Critic and philosopher and poet unite in assigning to "the poor player" a seat in the triumvirate of the world's greatest thinkers. In the very slag and cinder of his volcanic genius lie embedded precious bits of moral truth and sparkling gems of thought, but his greatest creations have become our ideals of philosophy and art.

Time forbids that I should enter here on any extended discussion of the characteristics of the man Shakespeare and of his genius. But it is a pleasant thought that enough of him is known to leave the image of a calm and genial man, whose broad humanity was lit up by the sunshine of a cheerful, happy temper. His intellect was subtle, playful, and capacious; and Coleridge told but half the tale when he named him "the myriad-minded." In the radiant circle of Elizabethan dramatists, each a star of the first splendor, he was the central sun. He is the greatest of English poets.

The Elizabethan drama was the natural outgrowth of previous literary and social conditions, and the highest legitimate embodiment of the poetry of the age. It was not an accidental or conventional mode of expression with Shakespeare and his contemporaries, but the normal, necessary and spontaneous image of their minds. With his grand imagination, his all-embracing sympathy with man and nature, and his wonderful and intuitive insight into the human heart, he was enabled, in his own language, "to hold, as 'twere, the mirror up to nature; to show virtue her own feature, scorn her own image, and the very age and body of the time his form and pressure." Thus Shakespeare's peculiar gift is not to analyze, not to describe, but to reflect, as the polished crystal, all that passes before its magic surface. As you look therein the phantom passions and spectral imaginings which have haunted the habitations of your own heart rise in visible form to warn, to ennoble, and to redeem it. The guilty Lady Macbeth cries to her lord:

> "Your face, my thane, is as a book where men
> May read strange matters."

Your hearts, my hearers, are as a book writ with stranger matters still; and this master-magician holds it up that you may read therein.

The great poet uses his mother tongue as an instrument of such volume, range, and melody that his readers are continually tempted to string those pearls of language, which we call "the beauties of Shakespeare." And yet this is but his smallest function. It is as psychologist, philosopher, and master of the problems of the human heart that we must regard him, as we reverently approach the study of his mighty tragedies.

The dramas of Shakespeare make up a psychology none the less complete because it is concrete in its forms. Opinions vary as to which is the greatest of his works. But this is a question of little practical moment. In each, the form and the play of thought are exactly fitted to the spiritual conception which is the central idea of the drama. In the skill and subtlety with which the moral powers and manifold intellectual activities of man are manifested to the mind's eye, and in the philosophy of life, Hamlet is peerless and perennial. And still other plays of the master-workman evince his versatility, resources, and imagination, and his complete control over the materials, methods, and instrumentalities of his magic art. But Macbeth is his greatest poem.

That I am not unsupported in this position, I quote Hallam, who says: "The majority of readers, I believe, assign to Macbeth the pre-eminence among the works of Shakespeare; many, however, would rather name Othello, and a few might prefer Lear to either. The great epic drama, as the first may be called, deserves, in my own judgment, the post it has attained, as being, in the language of Drake, 'the greatest effort of our author's genius, the most sublime and impressive drama which the world has ever beheld.'" Nor are Drake and the judicious Hallam alone in this opinion. Campbell, in his life of Mrs. Siddons, says: "I regard Macbeth, upon the whole, as the greatest treasure of our dramatic literature." Gervinus, the great German commentator, says: "It stands forth uniquely pre-eminent in the splendors of poetic and picturesque diction, and in the living representation of persons, times, and places."

Whether Macbeth is the greatest of Shakespeare's plays or not, I think there can be no doubt that it is his greatest poem. This is the more remarkable as it is probable from internal evidences that it never received the finishing touches so necessary for the perfection of a work of art, but stands like some colossal statue—the dream of a seer—the stupendous outline of a great soul-study, conceived in its entirety in the mind of the artist. We discover gaps in the plot, confusion in the metaphor, details half completed, and a lack of those final thoughts which, like sweetest roses before a killing frost, blossomed forth in his last version of Hamlet. But this very incompleteness compels us, as it were, to enter the charmed circle of the poet's imaginings, view the author's mind in the processes of creation, and share with him in the solemn mystery of the production of this grand drama.

It may be, as Swinburne suggests, "that the sole text we possess of Macbeth has not been interpolated, but mutilated." He describes it as "piteously rent and ragged and clipped and garbled in some of its earlier scenes; the rough construction and the poltfoot metre, lame sense and limping verse, each maimed and mangled subject of players' and printers' most treasonable tyranny contending as it were to seem harsher than the other." Yet, along with the wise and deep-seeing authors before cited, this most musical of critics tells us, "But if Othello be the most pathetic, King Lear the most terrible, Hamlet the subtlest and deepest, work of Shakespeare, the highest in abrupt and steep simplicity of epic tragedy is Macbeth."

In the spirit of this suggestion I am prepared to admit that Macbeth *may be* (for I dread dogmatism) rather the torso of some masterpiece of our dramatic Phidias than the uncompleted ideal of his tragic muse. But dropping metaphor the greatness of the events, the rapidity of the action, the compression of the thought, the fervor of the diction, and the simplicity and directness of the moral movement, render it a noble example of tragic art. Macbeth is not only, as Hallam called it, the great epic drama, but also the great heroic drama. The action is shrouded in mysterious gloom, or lurid with an unholy supernatural light; the persons of the drama move in shadow, vast, sombre and majestic, like beings of some older and larger creation. As in the Iliad, Achilles, Ulysses, and Agamemnon deal with the Immortals, give the sword-thrust or receive the wound, so when Banquo and stout Macduff, the saintly Duncan and bloody Macbeth, enter the field of vision, the meaner race of mortals vanishes from sight. Hence the artistic effects of this play are not produced by nice gradations of shade, but by strong contrasts of color in scene, incidents, circumstance and character. The elements are in tumult; and the landscape, black beneath the lowering storm-cloud, is, nevertheless, belted with peaceful bands of sunshine. Fell murder and dire cruelty work out their purposes on innocence and loyalty, and final retribution is met "dareful, beard to beard" by defiant remorse. Macbeth, is indeed, a tremendous epic in dramatic form—an epic in the rush and swirl of its objective action, but a very pæan of subjective evolution struck from the fervid lyre of a heart white hot. But implicit within the folds of its royal drapery of poetry, indeed, at the very heart of its ancient legend, couches one of the problems of destiny—a mystery of the human soul—which we would do well to pluck forth, and lay bare to the scrutiny of our intelligence.

I have not selected this tragedy because its problem is the most difficult to solve, for, on the contrary, it is the most obvious ; but it is one of the grandest and most pathetic. It is the old story of temptation, crime and retributive justice. Hamlet and Macbeth were finished almost about the same time ; Hamlet, as an idea which had grown through a series of years and been worked out to its consummation ; and Macbeth, probably suggested by it, hurled from the crater of the author's imagination into the empyrean. Together they constitute the obverse and reverse of the heaven-stamped medal we call the human will. They are psychological complements of each other. In Hamlet the renunciation of the human will is balanced by the despotism of will in Macbeth. In Hamlet, "the courtier, soldier, scholar, the expectancy and rose of the fair state," is "quite, quite down"—and why? Because, a morbid conscience and irresolute heart keep his subtle intellect in play, until the moment for action has passed, and his vacillation overwhelms with ruin all his house. But the Thane of Glamis, audacious, merciless and prompt, closes with his opportunity, and on the instant puts his soul past surgery. All must bend or break before the energy of his tremendous will and his lawless lust of dominion. But Nemesis follows him too, and his crime works out its inevitable penalty.

But let us come now to the play itself, and consider

the material and web of the plot, and how its moral purpose is evolved. A mediæval legend from Holinshed's dry Chronicle furnishes the incidents of the story. Following this outline, but weaving into it striking features from other similar tales, the author wins the credence of his audience by an apparent adherence to historical fact; while his perfect dramatic instinct teaches him to produce the profoundest impressions by conforming these rigid materials to the standard of ideal, universal, essential truth. Here is the story of Macbeth : Duncan, the saintly, but feeble, King of Scotland, is assailed by rebellion and invasion, which are repelled by his two generals, Macbeth and Banquo, who win public commendation and the rewards of the King. While returning from victory, they meet upon a blasted heath the three Weird Sisters, who hail Macbeth as Thane of Glamis, Thane of Cawdor, and King of Scotland hereafter, and predict for Banquo that his offspring shall ascend the throne. Banquo's sturdy honesty rejects the bait, but Macbeth's restless ambition hovers around the unholy prediction. The messengers of the King meet him, and announce that the King has given him the titles and estates of the rebellious and vanquished Thane of Cawdor. Already, by inheritance, he was Thane of Glamis.

" Two truths are told, as happy prologues to the swelling act of the imperial theme."

A fiendish suggestion has planted in his breast a wicked thought. He entertains it there, and it gathers and grows into a purpose to fulfill the prophecy. While this is taking shape, a fatal hint infuses the poison of lawless ambition into the veins of his wife, and the "dear partner of his greatness" becomes the partner of his guilt. When he hesitates, she urges him to the execution of the crime, through which he will ascend the throne. He avails himself of a friendly visit of the King to murder him; and then, to conceal his own guilt, stabs the sleeping chamberlains. Duncan's sons, alarmed for their safety, fly. Macbeth charges them with the murder, and himself ascends the throne. His usurpation now seems established, and all goes well with him; but he cannot feel secure while Banquo lives, for Banquo witnessed his temptation and may profit by his crime, while his stainless integrity stands like a perpetual reproach to Macbeth's disloyalty and guilt. He must die. Banquo is waylaid and assassinated; but his "blood-boltered" ghost rises at a royal banquet to shake the soul of Macbeth with horror. In his desperate desire to search out the future, the murderous usurper seeks the witches, and, lured by their infernal lights, he butchers in cold blood the wife and children of Macduff, Thane of Fife, who has fled to the true prince, Malcolm, in England. But this cruelty does not prosper. Suspicion, hatred and horror follow him. His wife, pursued by remorse, kills herself. And at last, cheated by the fiends he trusted, the tyrant falls in battle by the hand of Macduff, and the son of the murdered Duncan ascends the throne. From these simple materials, the skilful hand and informing spirit of the great artist built up a royal palace in the realm of thought.

The felicity of Shakespeare's genius shows itself in

AND OTHER SHAKESPEARIAN PROBLEMS. 51

the selection of the time and place and plot of this tragedy. Surely, these are not accidents. The venue is laid in the border-land of fact and fable. Macbeth was a contemporary of that Edward the Confessor whose reign lingered for generations in the fancy of Saxon England as a golden age. It was to Shakespeare a heroic age; and the figures and events of his creation loom up loftily through twilight and mist, too large and vague perhaps, did not human passions so sharply define them.

But the place as well as the time of the drama evoke a vivid interest. Scotland, though neighboring, was yet almost unknown to Englishmen of that day, and a series of tragic events and the calamities of kings had just linked its history with that of England.*

---

*It has been ingeniously maintained, and not without considerable evidence, that Shakespeare visited in person the scene of the action in Macbeth. Among other curious proofs is a letter quoted in the Athæneum (No. 2830, January 21, 1882). This letter is published by Mr. Edward J. L. Scott.

BRITISH MUSEUM, Jan. 17, 1882.

I have lately come across (in a volume of correspondence between the English and Scotch courts during the negotiations for the marriage of James VI. and Anne of Denmark) a letter of surpassing interest as regards the whereabouts of Shakespeare between 1587, the date when he left Stratford enrolled as a member of Burbage's company of players, called the Queen's company, and 1591, the date of his beginning to write alone as an author (see Fleay's Shakespeare Manual, pp. 4 and 5).

The letter, which I here subjoin, is from Henry le Scrope, ninth Baron Scrope of Bolton, Governor of Carlisle and Warden of the West Marches, to William Asheby, English ambassador at the court of James VI.:

"After my verie hartie comendacion on a letter receyved from

James I. had but just come to the throne; and, to Southern eyes Scotland lay like a mountain lake, half robed in romance and half veiled in mystery. Under the enchanter's wand, this gloomy background faded into a land of shadows, the curtain of the unseen world was lifted, and the powers of the air mingled with human actors as persons of the drama.

The staple of the story, too, is not without strong parallelisms to events which had recently greatly excited the public mind. Earl Gowrie's conspiracy, aimed at the life of James I., was still fresh in the memories of men. The plots known as "the Main"

Mr. Roger Asheton, signifying unto me that yt was the kinges earnest desire for to have her majesties players for to repayer into Scotland to his grace;

"I dyd furthwith dispatche a servant of my owen onto them wheir they were in the furthest part of Langkenshire, wheropon they made their returne heather to Carliell, wher they are and have stayed for the space of ten dayes, wherof I thought good to gyve you notice in respect of the great desyre that the kyng had to have the same to come onto his grace; and withall to praye yow to give knowledg therof to his Majestie. So for the present, I bydd yow right heartilie farewell.

"Carlisle, the XXth of September, 1589.
"Your verie assured loving friend,
"H. SCROPE."

There is no further letter relating to the subject among Asheby's correspondence, but it is very interesting to think that Shakespeare visited Edinburgh at the very time when the witches were tried and burned for raising the storms that drowned Jane Kennedy, mistress of the robes to the new queen, and imperilled the life of Anne of Denmark herself.

Mr. Scott adds: "In that case the witches in "Macbeth" must have had their origin from the actual scenes witnessed by the player so many years previously to the writing of that drama in 1606."

and "the Bye," for the murder of the king and the enthronement of his cousin, Arabella Stuart, had lately occurred; and the trials of Sir Walter Raleigh and others had awakened the liveliest interest touching regicide and the breach of a clear title to the crown. If, as best conjectured, this play was completed early in 1606, then it came just on the heel of the Gunpowder Plot, which had been fixed for November 5th, 1605; and the trials of the wretched fanatics who had compassed the destruction of King and Parliament had made the popular mind familiar with projects of slaughter and the casuistry of assassination. Shakespeare's treatment of his theme commended itself not only to the prince, but to the people; and while he adapted it to the spirit of the age, and even to the passing mood of the public, he evinced his transcendent genius by producing a poem of perennial interest, the spectacle of a titanic nature utterly cast down and ruined in its great spiritual struggle. Neither in prologue, nor in epilogue, nor in the mouth of any interlocutor, does the author announce the moral of the play. Yet he who runs may read. It is the contest for the soul of a man. The powers of darkness wrestle with and vanquish him.

We can properly understand this tragedy only by first understanding its supernaturalism. To do this aright we must look at it from the author's standpoint. There is scarcely any subject in literature more fascinating than the study of post-mediæval supernaturalism as embodied in the plays of Shakespeare. This is an age and country of a skepticism so general and pervading that we find it hard to conceive of the immense mass of superstition which overlaid the Christianity of the Middle Ages. Folklore, the hierarchy of angels and demons, the realm of faery, the habits and manners of ghosts; witchcraft with its laws, customs, cultus, and criminal practices; auguries, oracles, sorcery and other manifestations of occult power; spells, talismans, elixirs, and alchemy conjuring with the unknown and unsubdued forces of nature; astrology and the influence of the stars; the meaning of dreams and visions; in a word the whole world of the unreal had been systematized into a complete code and body of supernatural mythology, believed alike by peasant and prince, by learned and unlearned, and by all classes of the community. Relics of this remain imbedded in our earlier literature, like flies in amber; and other relics still yet crop out in the fancies, the follies and the crimes of the present generation. This vast machinery of mythology, which then represented to the popular mind the secondary causes through which God governs his universe, seems to us but the kaleidoscopic phases of a disordered dream, a mirage, "an unsubstantial pageant." But to our ancestors it was as real and solid as the rock-ribbed earth.

In Shakespeare's day, the British people was in the prime of national manhood. The light was breaking, and the emancipated human intellect was waking from the dreams of a thousand years. The prophetic soul of Shakespeare accepted the popular beliefs as modes of expression, and employed them as symbols for the unseen forces of nature and spirit, in which dwell activities more potent than even superstition could conjure up. And it was through this high poetic and philosophic power, this eminent gift of imagination and understanding working together, that he produced the terrible and highly idealized conception of supernatural agency embodied in the Weird Sisters. These and Banquo's ghost, the apparitions, the omens, the air-drawn dagger, the mysterious voice, are but the signs and formulas through which he represents the problem of evil, with which Macbeth grapples, and which he solves to his own temporal and eternal ruin.

A canon of Shakespearian criticism, somewhat fanciful perhaps, has been advanced, that the first scene, or even the first words, of a play, will often strike the keynote of the entire action. In Macbeth, certainly, they have a curious significance. The enchanter waves his wand, and the tragedy begins. Where? "In a desert place," or "open place," as some will have it; "with thunder and lightning." Is it on land or sea, or do the witches "hover through the fog and filthy air?" Whether we picture it as a barren heath, or above the ferment of the deep, we know that "the secret, black and midnight hags" are gathered on the confines of hell, with the gates ajar. Amid the tumult of the elements, and the mutterings of familiar spirits, the ominous question is shrieked forth,

"When shall we three meet again?"

This is answered by these "juggling fiends," when they next appear as tempters of Macbeth. The fine, lyrical movement of the scene reaches its highest pitch in the diabolic suggestion of the chorus,

> "Fair is foul, and foul is fair."

This phrase symbolizes the reversal of the divine order of nature, the love of evil for its own sake, the unforgivable sin. That this is not a mere conceit is evinced by the very first words that Macbeth utters,

> "So foul and fair a day I have not seen."

This is the human response to the infernal suggestion, and points to the moral confusion which infects the fairest state of man. This cannot be accidental. It is but one instance among many in Shakespeare where the echo of the mysterious footfall of the future is heard by an inner sense, and the word of unconscious prophecy is uttered. By this I do not mean that those omens and prodigies cited after Duncan's death, nor the predictions of the witches, but something subtler, akin to the derided and dreaded presentiment of evil.

Attention has been called to Shakespeare's art in opening the play with words that are in fact a prelude to its action.

A curious illustration of the ineptitude of much of the comment and emendation of Shakespeare will be seen in the following extract from "Story's Conversations in a Studio." (Vol. 1, p. 94) showing how another poet can stumble as to this very opening.

"Nothing can be more absurd in many respects than Burger's translation of 'Macbeth.' Poet, though he was, he seems to have lost all sense of poetry or reason in this translation, in which, in fact, he so ludicrously travesties the original, that one cannot but smile at the absurdities he introduces. The fact is, that Burger, who was a very vain man, thought himself far superior to Shakespeare, and kindly assisted him, and eked out his shortcomings. Think of this opening in ' Macbeth' :—

'SOLDIER. Hold ! not in such a hurry, good sir.
GUARD. Now, then ?
SOLDIER. I prithee, what is it you will tell the king ?
GUARD. That the battle is won.
SOLDIER. But I have been lying.
GUARD. Lying rascal ! Then thou art indeed with thy wounds a desperate joker.

This is a literal translation of one of Burger's improvements to Shakespeare."

An instance of the dramatic second-sight mentioned above is exhibited in Duncan's comment on the account of Cawdor's repentant death :—

> " There's no art
> To find the mind's construction in the face ;
> He was a gentleman on whom I built
> An absolute trust—"

Just here the new Thane of Cawdor enters with murder and treason in his heart, interrupting the reflection, while the king verifies and exemplifies in his words and conduct the aphorism he has just uttered.

Again, where Banquo for the last time leaves the King, he says :

> "A heavy summons lies like lead upon me,
> And yet I would not sleep."

Here there is something more than meets the ear, for the next moment Macbeth, charged with murderous purpose, greets him. In act 1, scene 2, Duncan begins, "What bloody man is this?" On this Bodenstadt comments, "This word 'bloody' reappears on almost every page, and runs like a red thread through the whole piece. In no other of Shakespeare's dramas is it so frequent." Again, Macbeth, while plotting Banquo's murder, urges him to attend the banquet. "Fail not our feast," he says. Banquo's promise, "My Lord, I will not," is fulfilled in a sense unexpected by either, or by the reader, when his "blood-boltered" ghost rises at the appointed place to shake with horror the marble heart of merciless Macbeth. Our secret sins find us out. Retribution is the debt never repudiated. The devil keeps his appointments.

The manner in which our poet has portrayed the Weird Sisters is but a solitary proof among many how far he was superior in real moral insight to the greatest even of the great poets who are sometimes named with him. Milton, most learned and religious, most metaphysical and most musical of poets, conceives Satan as the archangel ruined, who wins our human sympathy by the dazzling sublimity of his superhuman pride and despair. But Shakespeare's clearer and nobler perception of the essential ugliness and deformity of sin compels him to strike nearer the truth. The Weird Sisters, who embody the idea of evil, are beastly and loathsome, as well as terrible.

The beings called in this tragedy "the Weird Sisters" are not the malignant, yet impotent, old witches against whom the royal demonologist levelled the statute of 1604. Nor are they mere abstractions, personifications of the wicked promptings of Macbeth's heart. Though "bubbles of the air," they are not "fantastical." Real essences, prompters of sin, ministers of the evil one, and, like the Scandinavian Valkyrias, "posters of the land and sea," they brood over fields of slaughter, stir the elements to strife, and derange the moral and material order of the world. Such tasks are the work of strong fiends; but, as if in illustration of the essential connection of all evil, they do its drudgery with zeal. They mix the hell-broth of foul, venomous things, inflict and gloat over pain and misery, and yet are full of petty spite and filthiness. They are tempters to sin and can produce human suffering; but they have no compulsion for the soul, and recoil baffled from the assault on innocence. When the Weird Sisters struck the chord of unlawful aspiration in the bosom of Macbeth, it swelled into a symphony of treason and murder. But no irresistible necessity constrained him. Not fate, but his own free will, determined his downward career. And this is shown in that consummate touch of art by which Banquo is placed by the side of Macbeth and subjected to similar temptations, yet preserves his integrity unsullied, and dies a martyr to his loyalty. The mousing owls of Satan, the revolting caricature of humanity in its possible degradation, have merely to offer Macbeth the vast suggestion, and its echoes reverberate through his hollow and arid heart, until unhallowed reverie **grows** into guilty intention, and this ripens into crime. Thomas a—Kempis says well:

"For first a bare thought comes to the mind; then a strong imagination; afterwards delight, and evil motion and consent." So was it with Macbeth. He withstood not the beginnings of evil, and the end was utter ruin.

A true conception of the character of Macbeth, in whose soul the strife is waged, is necessary to grasp the real purpose of the play. This we may learn from the estimate put upon him by the popular voice, by his intimates, and by her to whom he had revealed "the naked frailties" of his soul. His soliloquies, too, unlock secret chambers into which the observer looks with sidelong glances. There he discerns the difference between this man before and after temptation, which, at the last, is the immeasurable distance between innocence and guilt, between a soul under probation and a soul betrayed and lost.

When the play opens he was to his followers and peers, "brave Macbeth," "valor's minion," "Bellona's bridegroom." The King calls him "valiant cousin," "worthy gentleman," "noble Macbeth," "peerless kinsman." In his own words, he had

> "Bought
> Golden opinions from all sorts of people."

His wife, who thought she knew the man, says of him in her first soliloquy:

> "Yet do I fear thy nature.
> It is too full o' the milk of human kindness
> To catch the nearest way: thou would'st be great;
> Art not without ambition, but without

> The illness should attend it ; what thou wouldst highly,
> That wouldst thou holily ; wouldst not play false,
> And yet would'st wrongly win."

With full allowance for the energy of the speaker's passion and ambition, this careful analysis portrays a mixed character. Macbeth's own ideal of himself is lofty :

> "I dare do all that may become a man ;
> Who dares do more is none."

The air-drawn dagger and the voice that "cried to all the house," echoes of a conscience, startled and aghast, are proofs of an imagination both sensitive and magnificent, even were the thoughts not uttered in heroic vein. But then, again, this capacious nature is cankered by selfishness.

There is in Macbeth's language a very distinct individualization, characteristically Shakespearian. His conversation is marked by a direct energy and blunt brevity, not uncommon with men of action, used to command. Like a true master of fence, reticence is his guard. He comes to the point without parley, and keeps at bay his fellow-men. But, on the other hand, in self-communion, and in converse with that other self, his wife, his imagination lifts itself in widening circles, like the eagle's flight, to its pride of place. After the murder, he replies to the salutations of the Thanes :

> "Good morrow, both.
> MACDUFF.—Is the King stirring, worthy Thane?
> MACBETH.—Not yet.
> MACDUFF.—He did command me to call timely on him.
>   I have almost slipped the hour.

> MACBETH.—I'll bring you to him.
> LENNOX.—Goes the King hence to-day?
> MACBETH.—He does; he did appoint so."

And to Lennox's description of the night, he answers: "'Twas a rough night." An examination of the play will show that he maintains this manner of speech throughout.

It is worth while to note, how in the excitement of preparation for his last battle, the tone of Macbeth changes as he addresses one or another of the interlocutors. He contemptuously damns the "cream-faced loon" who shows fear, and flings a wrathful "Liar and slave" at the messenger who brings the bad news of Birnam Wood; to his last friend, his armor-bearer, Seyton, he pours out his heart in sympathetic and confidential frankness; and, in the next moment, engages the doctor, the man of learning, in an ironical, yet highly imaginative conversation.

His exalted imagination, his vaulting ambition and his nearness to the throne had lured his thoughts to forbidden fields. Haunted by the glories of the royal state, he saw within the circle of the diadem power and fame, and (such is human weakness) some vision of compensatory beneficence. And this view is countenanced by the Chronicle, which describes him as a just, vigorous and religious monarch. All this was embraced in his scheme of

> "Solely sovereign sway and masterdom,"

in the way of which only the feeble Duncan stood; Though Macbeth declares the first "supernatural soliciting" of the Weird Sisters, a

> "Suggestion
> Whose horrid image doth unfix my hair
> And make my seated heart knock at my ribs,
> Against the use of nature.'"

yet we find him presently contemplating himself as mounting the throne,

> "If chance will have me king, why chance may
> Crown me, without my stir.'"

A friend's mischance is to be the airy stepping stone from thought to deed. Macbeth nurses these 'black and deep desires." When he meets his wife after all his achievements, his first words are

> "My dearest love,
> Duncan comes here to-night;"

and hers,

> "And when goes hence?"

to which he significantly replies,

> "To-morrow—*as he purposes.*"

It is she who shapes the horrid thought in its completeness,

> "O never
> "Shall sun that morrow see."

There is a tremendous force of purpose in this short, strong phrase. Each word stands out like a boss upon an iron mace. Across this sombre hatching of conspiracy, the arrival of the saintly Duncan falls like a burst of sunshine. He pauses a moment before the castle gates in calm enjoyment of the fair aspect of the peaceful scenery. He says to Banquo:

> "This castle hath a pleasant seat; the air
> Nimbly and sweetly recommends itself
> Unto our gentle senses."

Banquo, with the same human eye, takes note of

"This guest of summer, the temple-haunting martlet,"

and briefly draws a picture of tranquil beauty. What an outlook of nature smiles upon us. Then, like the last rays of the setting sun, Duncan's innocence casts its beams upon the portals of that grim abode of conspiracy and sudden death. With absolute trust and courtly grace he enters the castle. The confiding gentleness with which he commits himself to the hands of his assassins is very touching.

But once within the sepulchral jaws of this treasonable den, and all is changed. Murder lurks in the murky air. No supernatural machinery is needed to show that here the fiends have mastery. The impulse has been given, and man's wickedness works out the plot. In a gray and vaulted hall, dimly we discern two figures whispering in shadow, and an air-drawn dagger,—"on its blade and dudgeon gouts of blood which were not so before"—and then,

"Methought I heard a voice cry, 'sleep no more,'
Macbeth does murder sleep."

Duncan lies murdered in his bed. Macbeth had made his choice, and henceforth to him,

"Fair is foul, and foul is fair."

But he had not done "the deep damnation of his taking off" on kinsman and king, without hesitation and debate. The progress and growth of evil is powerfully illustrated in the reaction of guilt by which Macbeth and his wife mutually urge each other onward and downward. He first touched the fatal spring of her ambition, and instantly her whole nature glowed with the cold intensity of the electric light. Then, when he seemed to vacillate before the threats of vanquished virtue and an awakened conscience, the spirit he has raised in the woman's bosom will not down, but lifts its serpent crest to taunt with hissing tongue, and lure and urge him relentlessly to the bloody deed. Her hard, cold, narrow and direct intellect sees no end but the diadem, no means but the dagger. Her unbending, yet feminine, wickedness employs every stratagem of diabolical rhetoric to hold him to his purpose; she knows him to be fearless, aggressive, audacious, and, with a purpose once fully formed, prompt and decisive. This was the temper which had made him so dauntless a soldier on the field, and so fortunate a commander. To fix that purpose in the contest between conscience and will, she combines a tremendous energy with fiendish subtlety. When he seems about to cast aside his dark design, she holds him to it by first suggesting it to him as *her* work, not his.

> "He that's coming
> Must be provided for; and you shall put
> This night's great business into *my* dispatch."

She knows him well; for, once resolved, he truly says:

> "I am *settled*, and bend up
> Each corporal agent to this terrible feat."

And so he is led on and on down the dark and winding stairway of death and hell.

While the poet's function in Macbeth was, as I have said, the evolution of a moral problem, and not specially the delineation of character, yet Shakespeare's absolute artistic perceptions would not permit him to portray a character inconsistent with itself. Did time permit, I could readily demonstrate this in each person of the drama. It is Shakespeare's special gift to condense a whole character and display it in a few words, as a flash of lightning, in blackest midnight, reveals a landscape.

Thus, while in Holinshed's Chronicle Banquo is Macbeth's accomplice, the poet, ennobling his character and idealizing his integrity, makes him serve a higher purpose. And so we find Banquo described by Macbeth, who says of him,

> "There's none but he
> Whose being I do fear."

And again,

> Our fears in Banquo
> Stick deep ; and in his royalty of nature
> Reigns that which would be feared :—'tis much he dares,—
> And to that dauntless temper of his mind,
> He hath a wisdom that doth guide his valor
> To act in safety."

Macduff, "noble, wise, judicious," "child of integrity," and full of "noble passion," yet is ever hasty and rash. The gracious and gentle Duncan suffers for his childlike trustfulness, while his son, the wary Malcolm, exhibits in every word and act the caution and worldly wisdom in which his father is deficient. His prudential virtues receive their proper temporal reward, while Duncan, sacrificed on the altar of his own credulity, wears the crown of martyrdom. Even in the subordinate characters of the play, we find this coherence, as in the queen's gentlewoman, who, in her reticence and propriety, is still ever a gentlewoman indeed.

But to my mind the nicest analysis and most careful synthesis could not so truly construct a wicked woman, as Shakespeare has created one in Lady Macbeth. The whole gamut of criticism has been run by the commentators in characterizing her. From the verdict of those, who, with the bereaved Malcolm, describe her as "the fiendlike queen," we may pass to the opposite view of the German critic, Leo. This profound pundit says of her, "the wife, on the other hand, at the side of a noble, honorable husband, always faithful to the right, would have been a pure and innocent woman diffusing happiness around her domestic circle, in spite of some asperities in her temper." Even this genial estimate cannot so far remove prejudice as to enable us to imagine Lady Macbeth as a pleasant person to have about the house. She is a typical murderess: yet she is a woman, not a fiend; a woman, and a queen.

We have seen her finishing the work of overthrowing Macbeth's conscience, which the Weird Sisters had begun. She *says* of Duncan,

"I could have stabbed him as he slept."

Yet she did not. There is a vast distance between intensity of desire and power of execution. Her feminine nature recoiled from the deed itself, though not from its contriving. Unlike Macbeth, she had seen no daggers, heard no voices; but she could not actually stab the sleeping Duncan. She excuses herself thus,

> "Had he not resembled
> My father as he slept, I had done't."

Mrs. Siddons, the dark-browed queen of tragedy, fancied that Lady Macbeth was "fair, feminine, nay perhaps even fragile," vaulting ambition kindling "all the splendors of her dark, blue eyes." But crime has no special complexion—blonde or brunette—no more than has female fascination.

She is guilty, but a queen, and retains, even under the shadow of her inexpiable sin, the lofty refinement of her birth and rank. In the horror and confusion of Duncan's death, she swoons. This is the turning point in her fate. Then the bubble of ambition burst. How hollow and delusive it all seems now.

> "Nought's had, all's spent,
> Where our desire is got without content;
> 'Tis safer to be that which we destroy
> Than by destruction dwell in doubtful joy."

At first, clinging to the last plank of human sympathy and love left from the wreck, she bends herself to the task of consoling her husband—but in vain. For herself, nothing is left but remorse. The stiff fibre of her pitiless heart had stretched too far—and broken; but not in repentance, only in the agony of a never-dying dread. The hand that a little water was to cleanse bears "a damned spot." She

> "Is troubled with thick coming fancies
> That keep her from her rest."

Walking in her troubled sleep, she cries:

> "What! will these hands ne'er be clean?
> Here's the smell of blood still; all

> The perfumes of Arabia will not
> Sweeten this little hand. O! O! O!"

Well may the doctor exclaim:

> "What a sigh is there! the heart is sorely charged."

Well might she wish herself with pious Duncan in his peace. At last there came a cry of women, and the Queen was dead.

At the point of Duncan's doom, Macbeth trembled, and his wife chided him as "infirm of purpose." But his man's nature was made of the sterner stuff. As he stepped from crime to crime, what with the swing of his sceptre and his angry work of repression, he became "bloody, bold and resolute." Baffled by juggling friends, betrayed by courtiers, and bereft of wife, his heart did not break, nor his brain become frenzied. He opposed himself, like a Titan, to the vengeance of heaven and the dread of hell— fear of man he never knew. The props of infernal prophecy sank under him, and yet he would not fly. Then, "championed to the utterance with fate," at the last he falls like a soldier, sword in hand, unrepenting and defiant.

The poetic justice which assigns awakened sensibility as a necessary part of the penalty of sin is incorrect. Macbeth displays a more usual form of punishment. A gradual hardening of the heart, a constant moral descent with neither ability nor wish to recall the lost innocence and an increasing catalogue of crimes ensue, until the whip of scorpions and the avenging Furies are needed to shake his obdurate soul. In him we learn that there is no disconnected sin, but that offences are the links in an endless chain, harnessing cause to remotest consequence, and dragging the guilt-burthened soul downward forever. We saw him at first, with "love, honor, obedience, troops of friends." And now, in their stead,

> "Curses not loud but deep, mouth-honor, breath,
> Which the poor heart would fain deny, and dare not."

It is thus that Satan fulfills his promises. Even in the moment of fruition, when success seemed to have justified his usurpation, he received a bitter foretaste of his awful future. Shakespeare does not palter with this aspect of crime. He fills the meed of temporal prosperity for the murderer, crowns him, surrounds his throne with obsequious courtiers, crushes his enemies, and gives him all—

> "Thou hast it now: King, Cawdor, Glamis, all,
> As the weird women promised."

But he does not give him one happy moment. Lady Macbeth says to him:

> "How now, my lord! why do you keep alone,
> Of sorriest fancies your companions making?"

He bewails that they must

> "Sleep
> In the affliction of the terrible dreams
> That shake us nightly; better be with the dead,
> Whom we, to gain our place, have sent to peace."

The moral isolation of Macbeth and his wife is marked from the moment of his crime. The fissure gradually widens until it becomes an abyss of distrust, hatred and revolt. The thanes fall away, the soldiers blench,

> "And none serve with him but constrained things,
> Whose hearts are absent too."

This moral isolation—this segregation from human sympathy—ends in the alienation of the guilty pair; and their mutual affection, once so tender, closes in cold disregard. Selfishness is the essence of sin, and in absolute selfishness it finds its consummation.

Macbeth is a tragedy indeed. It is the spectacle of a human soul, which, under no depostism of destiny, but in the exercise of a lawless will, accepts the bribe of the tempter, and thus makes a destiny for itself—the destiny of perdition. We see a man of might, with his feet planted on a rock. To win a gilded bauble he plunges into the sea. He is a strong swimmer in the arms of the whirlpool; but they are arms which will not give up their prey. The lesson of Macbeth is a sad and solemn one. It bids us look into the abysses of our own souls, lest therein may lurk some motive to tempt us to our doom. And it teaches this lesson by exhibiting a human soul—a grand heroic soul—tempted, struggling, betrayed, lost.

In the words of the Preacher, the son of David, King in Jerusalem: "Let us hear the conclusion of the whole matter: fear God, and keep His commandments: for this is the whole duty of man. For God shall bring every work into judgment, with every secret thing, whether it be good, or whether it be evil."

THE SIGNIFICANCE OF HAMLET.

> "You would pluck out the heart of my mystery."
> *Hamlet*, II., 2.

The republic of letters has its first, or central, place—its throne. Even if merely a primacy among peers, the suffrages of the world, howsoever irregularly ascertained, insist upon a First to fill it. Homer long enjoyed this distinction, and his Saturnian reign has its partisans; but English-speaking men will not have it so, and a new sovereign now sways the Olympus of thought and imagination— one Shakespeare—with the divinity that doth hedge a king. There are rebels who held out against this usurpation, but in vain. Dion Boucicault shows most ingeniously how much has been done for Shakespeare's reputation by play-actors, the "stars" of the stage. It may be so, but these stage triumphs are but one small fraction of his mighty influence on modern thought; one facet, among many, of the diamond that reflects back to the questions of philosophy, poesy and prudential common-sense, answers that are accepted as oracles, Delphic and divine.

The Baconian contention, rooted not in reasonable protest but in mere love of paradox, is really a compliment to Shakespeare. It presupposes that what he did was *impossible* to any but a genius of the highest order, with the best training, and with all the advantages of wealth, leisure and opportunity. And yet who was Homer? A blind nobody; though Wolf and the Wolfians, anticipating modern industry, would have him transformed into a poetical syndicate or Pan Hellenic Ballad Trust Company. The plays of Shakespeare, argue the Baconians, are too great to have been written by a mere play-writer; a philosopher must have done them; no less a one, indeed, than the mighty Bacon, powerful, subtle, aphoristic, could have produced such dramas. This Baconian-myth logic might make William M. Evarts the creator of Lord Dundreary, and Gladstone the only possible author of the Idyls of the King. The fundamental mistake in all this consists: first, in assigning all training to the schools; second, in deciding *a priori* where, on whom, and how, will descend the divine gift of genius. Shakespeare, however, did have just the training to fit him for this work, and Bacon did *not;* but, more than all, the same Providence who bestowed on Bacon acumen and breadth of view gave Shakespeare insight. The whole controversy implies, argues from, the fact of a master—a mighty thinker—as the author of these plays. Bacon's analysis went through the world of thought, clearing and classifying things with the sword of the spirit. He saw with clear perception their true relations, and the law which expressed their order. But his talents were other than those of the poor player who possessed the magic art of literary creation, who had received the gift of vision and of prophecy and tongues, and who could summon from the world of idea existences that have put on the garb of humanity and become immortal. Think of it, indeed; are not the persons of his drama more real, more distinct, than the personages who then strutted as the great, and believed that they were moving and moulding the world, but who are now to us mere faded phantoms, shadows in the lamentable past, extinguished candles, burnt to the socket, with some faint odor left of smoke and grease? But it is not to our purpose here to enter upon the great Baconian controversy, and we dismiss it until we have the final verdict of a court of last resort. We will *assume* William Shakespeare. Credo!

William Shakespeare, playwright, stage manager, prudent man of business, who didst bequeath thy *second best* bed, for reasons explicable in sentiment, to thy relict, whilom fair Anne Hathaway, stand forth and justify this thy preposterous claim to the primacy in the republic of letters! "Fair sirs, I make no claim. In my day, for bread and betterment, I wrought, doing what my hand found to do. I printed few books. True, I made plays, and gathered shells and seaweeds along the shore, wherewith the sons of men might beguile some idle hours —in thinking. And yet—and yet—it did sometimes seem to me that in me I had that which might have fathered all of poetry and all of philosophy. But the ocean was too vast, and thought—O, thought!—too wide, and so—"

But not thus, gentle spirit, can thy claim—or claim for thee—be set aside. Serenely mayest thou smile at all the angry war of words between the champions who would canonize and the contestants who would crucify thy personality. But thy cause is in safe charge; and even as Aaron and Hur stayed the hands of Moses, so shall Goethe and Coleridge uphold thine.

The inspiration which Goethe received from Shakespeare is thus described by him; speaking as Wilhelm Meister, he says:

"Yes! I cannot recollect that any book, any man, any incident of my life, has produced such important effects on me as the precious works to which by your kindness I have been directed. They seem as if they were performances of some celestial genius, descending among men, to make them, by the mildest instructions, acquainted with themselves. They are no fictions. You would think, while reading them, you stood before the unclosed awful books of Fate, while the whirlwind of the most impassioned life was howling through the leaves and tossing them fiercely to and fro. The strength and tenderness, the power and peacefulness of this man have so astonished and transported me, that I long vehemently for the time when I shall have it in my power to read farther.

"All the anticipations I have ever had regarding man and his destiny, which have accompanied me from youth upwards, often unobserved by myself, I find developed and fulfilled in Shakespeare's writings. It seems as if he cleared up every one of our enigmas for us, though we cannot say: 'Here or there is a word of solution.' His men appear like natural men, and yet they are not. These, the most mysterious and complex productions of creation, here act before us as if they were watches whose dial plates and cases were of crystal, which pointed out, according to their use, the course of the hours and minutes, while, at the same time, you could discern the combination of wheels and springs that turned them. The few glances I have cast over Shakespeare's world incite me, more than anything beside, to quicken my footsteps forward into the actual world, to mingle in the flood of destinies that is suspended over it, and at length, if I shall prosper, to draw a few cups from the great ocean of true nature, and to distribute them from off the stage among the thirsting people of my native land." Under which wonderfully mixed metaphor, the great German advanced an idea.

Coleridge writes thus: "I believe Shakespeare was not a whit more intelligible in his own day than he is now to an educated man, except for a few local allusions of no consequence. And I said he is of no age—nor, I may add, of any religion, or party, or profession. The body and substance of his works came out of the unfathomable depths of his own oceanic mind; his observation and reading, which were considerable, supplied him with the drapery of his figures." (Table Talk, vol. 6, p. 506.)

Great as was the genius of Shakespeare, his judgment was at least equal to it.

The sweeping nature of Coleridge's characterization of Shakespeare as the exponent of a world literature has been questioned on the broad ground that no such literature and no such character can or does exist, but that every writer and thinker being limited and conditioned by his age and country, by antecedent conditions and actual environment, can only reflect or embody a segment of a national and epochal literature. Of course we can all see that the arc of one man's genius does not, and cannot, include or encompass the entire circumference of humanity, but Shakespeare's point of observation seems nearer the centre than any other man's since St. Paul. We must not be too literal with Goethe and Coleridge, and men who use the vernacular, instead of scientific formulas. The truth is often larger than the fact, though it must contain it. The plane on which move such minds as Tennyson's, Spencer's and Gladstone's, and that on which crawls the glow-worm that serves the Australian savage, or the slum dweller of New York, for light of intellect, seem parallel, one in the empyrean, the other in the slime, but with no point of approach. And yet Shakespeare did conceive, create, Hamlet and Christopher Sly, Prospero and Caliban, Falstaff and Othello, and had learned the secret of intellectual reconciliation between phases of humanity the most diverse. So that, though it is true that in the "Roman citizens" of Coriolanus or Julius Cæsar we discover the London Mob, and no Romans ever had the opinions, or exact modes of thought, that Shakespeare portrays in them, still neither shall this concern us, for they had hearts and passions which bellowed forth rage or applause, in different idiom truly, but with the same pulsations that now stir all hearts. Surely it is not too much to call him the "many-minded." If not absolute, universal, as nothing human, finite, can be, yet, as touching profounder depths, revealing in clearest light deeper abysses, and embracing wider relations than any other, must we not fairly assign to Shakespeare a *quasi universality*, and such actual primacy, and even sovereignty, in the world of letters, as is gained by common consent and general suffrage?

If the first place in literature be assigned to Shakespeare, so, though not without dissent, the first place among his creations must be accorded to Hamlet. Admit that Macbeth is a grander poem, that in dramatic conception and execution Othello excels it, that Lear stirs blacker depths in the Stygian pool, that in the music of its cadences the Tempest beats with a finer rhythm, that in a dozen of his dramas he holds the mirror more squarely to the exterior realities of life around us, and that in Hamlet a hundred faults may be found, yet, after all, we say this is marvellous, this is the masterpiece of the master.

Strange that this should be so, as this play is, in form and conception, the least dramatic of Shakespeare's great plays. Many of its situations, it is true, are sufficiently striking to warrant its popularity with the groundlings as well as with the scholars and critics; but a bare comparison will show how inferior as an acting play it is in tragic movement to Macbeth, Richard III., and other tragedies, and notably to Othello, which that able and admirable critic and scholar, Professor Thomas R. Price of

Columbia college, has demonstrated, I may say, to be Shakespeare's best acting play.

Why Hamlet should be regarded as the paragon of plays is, indeed, perplexing, if we look merely to its defects and limitations. The plot, at bottom, is barbarous, inconsequent, incoherent; the action drags; the crisis is an anti-climax; the catastrophe not a consequence of the action, but of the want of action, "for this effect defective comes by cause," as pedantic Polonius says. And occult questions of life, death, immortality, free-will and fate propounded receive no reply, except the cruel answer of the Sphinx to those who failed to solve her riddles, the bloody enigma of the catastrophe — destruction. What, then, does it all mean? Why do we turn again and again to the melancholy Dane with such intense and sympathetic interest? Why ask with him the questions he has left unanswered? Because, in Hamlet the poet has bared a human heart. We look into its magic mirror and see our own hearts there.

While it is evident that Goethe, in the confidence of his own genius, felt able to improve on Shakespeare, and make a version of Hamlet better fitted to the wants of the stage at least, and while it is still more evident that in this estimate of his own powers he was mistaken, yet we must not forget the fact that to him more than to any one else is due a true method of interpretation of the master. With his powerful intellect, vivid imagination, and robust ethical sense, concentrated upon a kindred genius, even though higher and broader than his own, he was able, almost intuitively, to arrive at truths, which later, more learned and analytic, criticism has not been able to shake. We owe it to him that he arrested the thought of his century and compelled it to regard the great works of Shakespeare, not with a mousing and mechanical mental anatomy, but broadly, in the entirety of their conception, and from a spiritual point of view. If the following characterization of Hamlet be incomplete, erroneous indeed in part, as I think it is, yet in the extracts which follow, expository of the play, this first truly great commentator has been unsurpassed by his successors. He says:

"Soft, and from a noble stem, this royal flower had sprung up under the immediate influences of majesty; the idea of moral rectitude with that of princely elevation, that feeling of the good and dignified with the consciousness of high birth, had in him been unfolded simultaneously. He was a prince, by birth a prince; and he wished to reign, only that good men might be good without obstruction. Pleasing in form, polished by nature, courteous from the heart, he was meant to be the patron of youth and the joy of the world.

"He was calm in his temper, artless in his conduct, neither pleased with idleness nor too violently eager for employment. The routine of an university he seemed to continue at court. He possessed more mirth of humor than of heart; he was a good companion, pliant, courteous, discreet, and able to forget and forgive an injury, yet never able to unite himself with those who overstepped the limits of the right, the good, and the becoming."

"Calm" is certainly not the term to use of this restless intellect and eager heart; nor "artless," of a genius born for intrigue and full of all resources, except the direct way. In all the rest, the *Interpreter* seems to have read aright this wonderful character, but the subtlety of the prince has escaped, or beguiled, the search of the poet.

Goethe continues: "Figure to yourselves this youth, this son of princes; conceive him vividly; bring his state before your eyes, and then observe when he learns that his father's spirit walks; stand by him in the terrors of the night, even when the venerable ghost appears before him. He is seized with boundless horror; he speaks to the mysterious form; he sees it beckon him; he follows and hears. The fearful accusation of his uncle rings in his ears the summons to revenge, and the piercing, oft-repeated prayer, 'Remember me!'

"And, when the ghost has vanished, who is it that stands before us? A young hero panting for vengeance? A prince by birth rejoicing to be called to punish the usurper of his crown? No! trouble and astonishment take hold of the solitary young man; he grows bitter against smiling villains, swears that he will not forget the spirit, and concludes with the significant ejaculation:

> "'The time is out of joint; O, cursed spite,
> That ever I was born to set it right!'

"In these words, I imagine, will be found the key to Hamlet's whole procedure. To me it is clear that

Shakespeare meant, in the present case, to represent the effect of a great action laid upon a soul unfit for the performance of it. In this view the whole play seems to me to be composed. There is an oak tree planted in a costly jar which should have borne only pleasant flowers in its bosom; the roots expand, the jar is shivered.

"A lovely, pure, noble, and most moral nature, without the strength of nerve which forms a hero, sinks beneath a burden it cannot bear and must not cast away. All duties are holy for him; *the present is too hard.* Impossibilities have been required of him, not in themselves impossibilities, but such for him. He winds and turns, and torments himself; he advances and recoils; is ever put in mind, ever puts himself in mind; at last does all but lose his purpose from his thoughts, yet still without recovering his peace of mind.

* * * * * *

"It pleases us, it flatters us, to see a hero acting on his own strength, loving and hating at the bidding of his heart, undertaking and completing, casting every obstacle aside, and attaining some great end. Poets and historians would willingly persuade us that so good a lot may fall to man. In Hamlet we are taught another lesson; the hero is without a plan, but the play is full of plan. Here we have no villain punished on some self-conceived and rigidly accomplished scheme of vengeance; a horrid deed is done; it rolls along with all its consequences, dragging with it even the guiltless; the guilty perpetrator would, as it seems, evade the abyss made ready for him; yet he plunges in, and at the very point where he thinks he will escape and happily complete his course.

"For it is the property of crime to extend its mischief over innocence, as it is of virtue to extend its blessings over many that deserve them not; while frequently the author of the one or of the other is not punished or rewarded at all. Here is this play of ours, how strange! The pit of darkness sends its spirit and demands revenge, in vain! All circumstances tend one way and hurry to revenge, in vain! Neither earthly nor infernal thing may bring about what is reserved for fate alone; the hour of judgment comes; the wicked falls with the good; one race is moved away that another may spring up."

While such is Goethe's view, since reflected and refracted in half a hundred German mirrors, Karl Werder[*], in a very ingenious and able argument, has adopted a theory directly contrary to it. According to this theory, Hamlet's will was not at fault, but the situation made it morally impossible for him to obtain a proper vengeance by killing the King. He was more or less convinced of Claudius's guilt, but he had no evidence except the revelation of the Ghost, who could not be produced to prove his own assassination and the innocence of Hamlet, brought to trial as a parricide and regicide. The crime was improbable; the proof of it impossible. Werder argues that his object was not to kill Claudius but to force him to confess, or display, his guilt, and that he pursued this purpose constantly, and by the best means possible. Moreover, he insists that

[*] Furness' Variorum Hamlet, II., 354.

the drama moves rapidly to this conclusion. He fixes as the turning point in the play Hamlet's mistake in swerving from his purpose when he kills Polonius, after which event he is powerless. But the King, as the second person in the piece, then takes upon himself the solution of the knot, by action, and thus brings ruin upon his own head; so that, at last, guilt works out its own retribution, and secret crime comes to light. All this, and much more, is carefully argued with much subtlety of reasoning, but after all with more speciousness than solidity. It is the elaboration of paradox. How does common-sense view it? Shakespeare and his audience realize that a great crime has been committed, and that "Hamlet, Revenge!" is the burden of the theme. Much that Werder says is true, though not altogether new. Claudius was not a usurper in any proper sense, but held a legal title as King Consort, and his slaughter, without more ado, was not, dramatically-speaking, possible. But, if Hamlet's purpose was to make manifest his guilt, which we may for argument's sake admit, surely the worst way possible was to attempt to entrap him into a confession. And, moreover, there is little in the language of the interlocutors to favor such a theory, for the play of Gonzago is too thin a device to rest a hypothesis upon; while Hamlet's continuous whetting of his purpose to kill the King, and the ghost's supernatural invocation to the deed in the 4th act show that the poet's conception of Hamlet's mission was the punishment of the murderer. For instance, Hamlet says, "I say, we will have no more marriages : those that are married already, *all but one*, shall live : the rest shall keep as they are."

Mr. W. W. Story, a very competent and pleasant critic, pointing out the weakness of German criticism on Shakespeare, says : "Even Goethe's 'Analysis of Hamlet,' much as it has been praised, seems very poor to me—not to be mentioned for insight and sympathetic sense with, for instance, Lamb, Coleridge, or Hazlitt." While this is true, it must be remembered that they had the benefit of Goethe's interpretation before them, and the powerful aid of a common mother tongue and the same national instincts to guide them in comprehending the author.

And though the Analysis is full of obvious errors and incoherences, a step in the dark toward truth, it does not deserve Story's censure, that it is "boring and mechanical," for it struck the true keynote for all the rest. But it is true that one very signal defect in German criticism of Shakespeare is the want of perspective. Story says truly, "The Germans have the vice of anatomizing Shakespeare, and laying him out into parts and pieces, and admiring the worst as much as the best. They find admirable reasons to show that the notoriously ungenuine parts of his plays are as admirable as the others. When they once go in to praise, they praise everything."

Hear, however, what Coleridge says : "I believe the character of Hamlet may be traced to Shakespeare's deep and accurate science in mental philosophy. Indeed, that this character must have some connection with the common fundamental laws of our nature may be assumed from the fact that Hamlet has been the darling of every country in which the literature of England has been fostered. In order to understand him, it is essential that we should reflect on the constitution of our own minds. Man is distinguished from the brute animals in proportion as thought prevails over sense; but in the healthy processes of the mind, a balance is constantly maintained between the impressions from outward objects and the inward operations of the intellect:—for if there be an overbalance in the contemplative faculty, man thereby becomes the creature of mere meditation, and loses his natural power of action. Now, one of Shakespeare's modes of creating characters is to conceive any one intellectual or moral faculty in morbid excess, and then to place himself, Shakespeare, thus mutilated or diseased, under given circumstances. In Hamlet he seems to have wished to exemplify the moral necessity of a due balance between our attention to the objects of our sense, and our meditation on the workings of our minds,—an *equilibrium* between the real and the imaginary worlds. In Hamlet this balance is disturbed: his thoughts, and the images of his fancy, are far more vivid than his actual perceptions, and his very perceptions, instantly passing through the *medium* of his contemplations, acquire, as they pass, a form and a color not naturally their own. Hence we see a great, an almost enormous, intellectual activity, and a proportionate aversion to real action, consequent upon it, with all its symptoms and accompanying qualities. This character Shakspeare placed in circumstances, under which it is obliged to act on the spur of the moment:—Hamlet is brave and careless of death; but he vacillates from sensibility, and procrastinates from thought, and loses the power of action in the energy of resolve. Thus it is that this tragedy presents a direct contrast to that of Macbeth; the one proceeds with the utmost slowness, the other with crowded and breathless rapidity.*

"Hamlet's character is the prevalence of the abstracting and generalizing habit over the practical. He does not want courage, skill, will, or opportunity; but every incident sets him thinking; and it is curious, and, at the same time, strictly natural, that Hamlet, who all the play seems reason itself, should be impelled, at last, by mere accident, to effect his object. I have a smack of Hamlet myself, if I may say so." (*Table Talk* Vol. 6., p. 285.)

Lowell carries forward and develops these ideas of Goethe and Coleridge when he says, "Hamlet knows only too well what 'twere good to do, but he palters with everything in a double sense: he sees the grain of good there is in evil, and the grain of evil there is in good, as they exist in the world, and, finding that he can make those feather-weighted accidents balance each other, infers that there is little to choose between the essences themselves. He is of Montaigne's mind, and says expressly that 'there is nothing good or ill, but thinking makes it so.' He dwells so exclusively in the world of ideas that the world of facts seems trifling, nothing is worth the while; and he has been

---

* Notes on Hamlet, Complete works, Coleridge, vol. IV., p. 144 (Harper Bros., 1858.)

so long objectless and purposeless, so far as actual life is concerned, that, when at last an object and an aim are forced upon him, he cannot deal with them, and gropes about vainly for a motive outside of himself that shall marshall his thoughts for him and guide his faculties into the path of action. He is the victim not so much of feebleness of will as of an intellectual indifference that hinders the will from working long in any one direction. He wishes to will, but never wills. His continual iteration of resolve shows that he has no resolution." (*Lowell's Among my Books, p.* 214.)

"If we must draw a moral from Hamlet, it would seem to be, that Will is Fate, and that, Will once abdicating, the inevitable successor in the regency is Chance. Had Hamlet acted, instead of musing how good it would be to act, the king might have been the only victim. As it is, all the main actors in the story are the fortuitous sacrifice of his irresolution. We see how a single great vice of character at last draws to itself as allies and confederates all other weaknesses of the man, as in civil wars the timid and the selfish wait to throw themselves upon the stronger side." (*Lowell's Among my Books*, p. 225).

Why is the play of Hamlet what it is, and not something else? This has long been a question for the critics. The fundamental idea, the principle that directed the action and produced the situations of the play, has been eagerly sought by scores of commentators, who have hinged it upon this or upon that theory of Hamlet's character or condition, whence all the rest is logically derived.

To collate or review the manifold methods of interpretation of this tragedy adopted by commentators, except in a summary way, is not to my present purpose. One will have us believe that Shakespeare is striving to reproduce realistically a picture of that rude Viking life referred to in the legend of Saxo Grammaticus, on which the play is founded; and this, though the historic sense and historic perspective are modern, even recent, and Shakespeare, who was a psychologist, not a scientist, wore his array of facts as loosely as Hamlet his sable mantle. Among the Germans, and, for that matter, among certain Americans also, it is not uncommon to represent Shakespeare as anticipating with prophetic ken some later development of metaphysics or philosophy, and illustrating it in his dramas. Now he is a Neo-Hegelian in the third stage of consciousness, and, interpreting him according to the formulas, we are called upon to read through the thin veil of word-play and plot the final facts of Being prefigured in his types :—and, if they are not there, so much the worse for Shakespeare. Or, again, an ingenious Max-Mullerite, or G. W. Coxologist, discovers that Hamlet is the unravelling of some Norse saga, the hatching of a myth egg laid in the Dawn of History, in the primeval past. Carl Karpf offers us this exquisite gem of criticism : Hamlet's father, "Orvandell, (the Frozen Toe), the *chilblain*, is as the lightning spark, the hypostasis of Thor."

Furness, in his invaluable Variorum edition, gives us a complete mine of these dissentient opinions ; some grave and well considered, many most whimsical and fantastic.* Roetschl (II. p. 294) tells us, that "in Hamlet, Shakespeare has, like a prophet, seized the nature of the German character in its deepest significance. Hamlet's strength and weakness are the strength and weakness of the German people." Freiligrath, begins a poem, beautifully translated by Mrs. Wistar (p. 379): "Yes, *Germany* is Hamlet!" Sievers (p. 223) says: "We ourselves trust in the sequel to prove that this drama is intended to represent the peculiar, fundamental principle of Protestantism." He says also: "What the poet here represents is the torture and weakness of a nature that has fallen out with the world, and lost its hold : it is the break of the consciousness which robs the soul of faith, and renders it incapable of all self-forgetting devotion, of all elevation above self. The great Protestant idea of man's need of faith, of faith as the condition of his peace, and the fulfilment of his mission as a moral being, this it is to which this profoundest and most moving of all the works of Shakespeare's genius owes its origin." While such a conclusion may possibly be implicit somewhere in the teachings of this drama, it assuredly requires a most strained interpretation to set it out as the original purpose or as the fundamental principle, which Shakespeare intended to represent in it. Rohrbach (p. 306) says, "That Shakespeare meant to portray in Hamlet a sickly talking hero." Again, we have found Werder picturing him as a man ever ready to strike, to cut the Gordian knot. He tells us, "The

* Quotations not otherwise marked are from Furness' Hamlet, 2d vol.

piece knows no delay." One man, Dr. Benedix, (p. 351) regards the whole play as a bungling mistake. And Moriz Rapp (p. 295) comes to the conclusion, "that the scheme of the work was from the beginning wrongly contrived, i.e., undramatically." Play-goers and thinkers have thought otherwise.

Voltaire says of Hamlet, that "it is a vulgar and barbarous drama that would not be tolerated by the vilest populace of France or Italy." "One would imagine this piece to be the work of a drunken savage."

Froude points out very well the ineptitude and incongruity of much of the criticism and alteration of Shakespeare in the following passage :

"Cibber and others, as you know, wanted to alter Shakespeare. The French king, in Lear, was to be got rid of; Cordelia was to marry Edgar, and Lear himself was to be rewarded for his sufferings by a golden old age. They could not bear that Hamlet should suffer for the sins of Claudius. The wicked king was to die, and the wicked mother ; and Hamlet and Ophelia were to make a match of it, and live happily ever after. A common novelist would have arranged it thus ; and you would have had your comfortable moral that wickedness was fitly punished, and virtue had its due reward, and all would have been well. But Shakespeare would not have it so. Shakespeare knew that crime was not so simple in its consequences, or Providence so paternal. He was contented to take the truth from life ; and the effect upon the mind of the most correct theory of what life ought to be, compared to the effect of the life itself, is infinitesimal in comparison."

Chateaubriand, whom some people consider himself somewhat shallow and showy, speaks of Hamlet as: "This tragedy of maniacs, this royal bedlam in which every character is either crazy or criminal, in which feigned madness is added to real madness, and in which the grave itself furnishes the stage with the skull of a fool, etc."

All which shows that tastes differ, and that the yardstick of French, or even German, philosophy and criticism is not the measure for the orbed genius of the greatest of poets.

The question so often started, so much and so ably discussed, of Hamlet's madness seems to be hardly a question at all, though each critic has his theory. Hamlet says he will *feign* madness; and, even when so feigned, it is most doubtful to the persons of the drama, and should not be so at all to the audience. The whole thing seems to turn upon a play upon words. If we are all mad, as some allege, Hamlet was mad. Was he then sane? If sanity means perfect health of mind, body and soul, surely not. Who is? Certainly we have here a soul in sore distress, a willow bending before the storm of life, bending this way and that, even as old saws advise, and yet at last wrenched from its rooted bed and swept into utter vacuity and failure, because it obeyed the law of its being and was a willow and not an oak? Yet oaks, too, go down before tempests sent for their rending, even as willows are torn up when the hurricane strikes them. The resistance of the one or of the other is merely a measure of the force of the tornado. But, willow or oak, Hamlet was not equal to "the blast from Hell" he encountered.

We must remember, too, that, in the old legend, Hamlet's madness was but put on, for a purpose. And if Shakespeare makes it real, not feigned, what lesson are the sound in mind to draw from it? Ophelia's madness was real; if Hamlet's also, then would we have upon the stage the counterplay of a mad hero and a mad heroine—"a mad world, my masters;" Bedlam brought home to us as the picture of mankind. That noble and majestic reason was harshly wrung no doubt, but not overthrown. If the scenes of this drama are but pictures of lunacy, its moral purpose might be as well subserved by a book of dreams, the shuffled cards dealt by Incubus to the sleeping.

I have shown how the commentators ring the changes on every crotchet and conceit that may be imagined. But, after all, it is to Goethe that we owe the clue that has led to the solution of the question, first and last, of the significance of Hamlet. Was not Goethe right (p. 333) when he says: "They come and ask me what idea I meant to embody in my Faust? As if I knew and could tell! To depict the reign of love, of hatred, of hope, or despair, and whatever the states and passions of the soul may be, is native to the poet, and it is his success simply to represent them."

Does Shakespeare, indeed, intend at all in Hamlet, to propound a theory, to elucidate a fundamental principle? Not perhaps as a formula, but surely in concrete human form. There is in it a man and an idea. Is it not the true solution of the entire mystery, that Shakespeare meant to portray a Man, the greatest of all the mysteries of creation—with what lesson we may derive from that man's failure? The Prince of Denmark is not an epitome of the virtues and vices, but a man, a real man, a human soul in contest with fate. We mount with him, and tread the airy paths of the spirit; with him we look into the seething depths of our natures and see suggested there, in Hamlet's indecision and abdication of the issue of events to circumstance, the defeat of the human will in its war with destiny, and that aspect of our being, which, however insoluble, forever stares at us—the very Gethsemane of the finite soul, the impotence of man in the world of spirit. This is the chief value, this the perennial interest, this the real significance of this wonderful drama.

Hamlet and Macbeth are, as has been often shown, the complements of each other in the tragic presentation of one of the most momentous questions that ever engaged the mind of man—that of the personal responsibility of the individual for his actions. Each of these plays propounds this problem for our solution after its own fashion. There are different ways of putting and answering questions. Socrates had his way, a most unfair one truly, however skilful and delightful. So they may be put and answered in sermons or in squibs? Shakespeare put his in stage plays, and answered them in enigmas. This great question of Fate and Free Will, or some aspects of it, he debates in both Hamlet and Macbeth. Answer, Macbeth, in thine own way, and thou, Hamlet, in

thine. Take thy unhallowed will, like the image of
a false god, Macbeth, into the temple of thy soul, and
pass through the fire to Moloch. And, thou, Hamlet,
cast thy purposes like jetsam from a struggling ship,
upon the waste of waters, and leave thy helm to play
of wind and wave, and the hulk shall drift till the remorseless sea devour all. Macbeth teaches the primal duty of rectitude of will; Hamlet, of decision of
will. The former rebukes the vacillation which hesitates between right and wrong, the latter the vacillation between action and procrastination. Macbeth
says, "Shall I do it, right or wrong?" Hamlet, "Right
or wrong, I cannot do it?" Each pays the penalty of
his sin. The claim, the right, the obligation, the necessity, in the scheme of Providence, of the energetic
exercise of a free will is the grand ethical and theological lesson taught in Hamlet. This is its lesson
for all men, as I have striven heretofore to explain;
but that Shakespeare intended it originally for a narrower and more special and personal scope and
application I think is most probable, and this I shall
endeavor to show hereafter in these lectures.

Without citing the libraries which have been written on Hamlet, the quotations I have given from
some of the grandest thinkers of modern times
evince the influence of the play and its creator upon
the world of thought. Its germ of Doubt has become
a full blown skepticism: its individual scrupulosity
a widespread habit of mind. This is curiously illustrated in the Journal of Amiel, translated by the
gifted author of Robert Elsmere, who seems to have
found in the Swiss professor the prototype for at least

two of her characters. Hamlet was intended as a warning against hesitation; Amiel saturates himself with Hamlet, and, as Hamlet, becomes hesitation incarnate.

Amiel says, 8th Nov. 1852, "Responsibility is my invisible nightmare. To suffer through one's own fault is a torment worthy of the lost, for so grief is envenomed by ridicule, and the worst ridicule of all, that which springs from shame of oneself. My privilege is to be the spectator of my own life drama, to be fully conscious of the tragi-comedy of my own destiny—that is to say, to be unable to take my own illusions seriously, to see myself, so to speak, from the theatre on the stage, or to be like a man looking from beyond the tomb into existence;" and much more to the same effect. He tells us, "Shakespeare must have experienced this feeling often, and Hamlet must express it somewhere." So Amiel, neglecting the purpose of the poet and the moral of the play, and fascinated by the opium dream of vacillation in Hamlet, spent thirty years in "craven scruple of thinking too precisely on the event," making small mark upon his time, and left for legacy some cloud-work of introspective psychology, and for warning his failure in life's purpose. Hamlet's influence on the life of this man, who extorts a languid admiration, may be illustrated by the following extracts from his Journal, which are curiously illustrative.

"6th July, 1853. "Why, in general, am I better fitted for what is difficult than for what is easy. Always for the same reason. I cannot bring myself to move freely, to show myself without a veil, to act on my own account and act seriously, to believe in and assert myself, whereas a piece of badinage which diverts attention from myself to the thing in hand, from the feeling to the skill of the writer, puts me at my ease. It is timidity which is at the bottom of it. There is another reason too,—I am afraid of greatness, I am not afraid of ingenuity, and, distrustful as I am of my gift and my instrument, I like to reassure myself by an elaborate practice of execution. All my published literary essays, therefore, are little else than studies, games, exercises, for the purpose of testing myself. I play scales, as it were; I run up and down my instrument, I train my hand, and make sure of its capacity and skill. But the work itself remains unachieved. My effort expires, and, satisfied with the power to act, I never arrive at the will to act. I am always preparing and never accomplishing, and my energy is swallowed up in a kind of barren curiosity—these are the two obstacles which bar against me a literary career. Nor must procrastination be forgotten. I am always reserving for the future what is great, serious, and important, and meanwhile I am eager to exhaust what is pretty and trifling." This is a long draught of Amiel, and I would not indulge myself in parading what may, in one sense, be but the morbid masking of a recluse, out worn with self-contemplation; but every close student of Hamlet will recognize in this self-portraiture an able and critical study, an exact portrayal, of the mind of Hamlet. The disciple had lost himself in his master.

Again Amiel tells us : "Every situation is an

equilibrium of forces ; every life is a struggle between opposing forces working within the limits of a certian equilibrium." "The man who insists upon seeing with perfect clearness before he decides, never decides." "·I am always trifling with the present moment. Feeling in me is retrospective. My refractory nature is slow to recognize the solemnity of the hour in which I actually stand. An ironical instinct, born of timidity, makes me pass lightly over what I have, on pretence of waiting for some other thing at some other time . . . . . I trifle even with happiness out of distrust of the future." These instances could be multiplied to any extent : but it is Hamlet, not Amiel, we have to deal with, and it is only because Amiel was a Hamlet in actual life, painting his prototype, while trying to photograph himself, that we reproduce and dwell upon his words so fully here.

As with Amiel the Genevese, so with Goethe and the German host who have enlisted under the banners of Hamlet ; to all these, and to thinkers and dreamers everywhere, the tragedy of Hesitation has o'ertopped the tragedy of Action. Hamlet reigns. Pontius Pilate washed his hands, saying, "I am innocent of the blood of this just person": but all the waves of the ocean and all the tides of time will not wash his soul clean from the blood-guilt he incurred when he refused to do what he knew was right. We cannot avoid the responsibility of action by delay, or words of renunciation.

In Hamlet, Shakespeare's fundamental canon of dramatic construction, organic unity in the action, is *apparently* violated, but not really so. The conditions which ordinarily lead to a sin of commission culminate here in a sin of omission. The interest is maintained up to the crisis, which consists, not in a fatal decision of the hero, but in a fatal indecision. It is the prince's failure to act, to do, at the point of fate, what the audience has a right to expect him to do, that culminates in—procrastination. His defect of will is the crisis. He lets slip his opportunity, and evades the appointed task. He shirks his responsibility, and pursues a waiting policy. His is a Fabian campaign, a sort of generalship, which, successful once in history, has served since as the apology for a thousand military abortions. In the latter half of Hamlet, the action is necessarily inconsequential. As the crisis consisted in an abdication of volition, it could have no consequences. Anarchy ensued in the moral government of the situation, until Fate, taking up the abandoned sceptre, decided a cause whose arbitrament belonged properly to the realm of the human will. What redeems this part of the play is the succession of brilliant stage situations springing from the intrigue and involutions of plot, together with the splendid lights and shades of a soul displayed under the electric glow of Shakespeare's psychology.

And yet we are not to believe that this movement in Hamlet is any more a mistake, or less profound, than that which dictates the *motif* of some grand operatic performance. A believer in Shakespeare's keen common-sense, his mastery of the theatre in all its aspects, and his artistic and literary insight, will not concede that the rhythm of the action in Hamlet is an accident even, or that the suspense, the ebb and flow of the tragic tide, and the unexpectedness—the lightning bolt—of the royal calamity, Æschylean in its final inevitableness, are other than parts of a purpose, the harmony of perfect art. The master knew what he was about, and, to produce desired effects, used the right means to the proposed end, putting aside all others.

I have said that in the unfolding of this great drama of fate and free-will, Shakespeare taught his lesson by bringing within range of our mental vision the soul of a man. This is the true solution ; and, when we say a man, we mean a particular man, not man—a type, a generalization, an abstraction, a phantasy, which never existed, and never will. But what man? It has been often said, and well said, that, in Hamlet, Shakespeare turned out his own soul for the study of the world. Kreyssig (p. 302) declares that, "From the rich troop of his heroes, Shakespeare has chosen Hamlet, as the exponent, to the spectators and to posterity, of all that lay nearest to his own heart."

Kenny (p. 177) beautifully expresses a thought more or less clearly shadowed by many others: "Hamlet is, in some sense, Shakespeare's most typical work. In no other of his dramas does his highest personality seem to blend so closely with his highest genius. It is throughout informed with his skepticism, his melancholy, his ever-present sense of the shadowiness and the fleetingness of life." But perhaps Hazlitt more clearly strikes the keynote when he says, (p. 155), "It is *we* who are Hamlet."

In "Hamlet's Traits of Character," "by a No Philosopher" (p. 351), the correct view of Shakespeare's mode of literary production herein is well set forth. "It is not in Hamlet, as in other pieces of Shakespeare's, the history of a single passion, the development of a few mental qualities, good or bad, that is set before us. In this drama Shakespeare sets himself a greater task; to make clear and intelligible from the whole structure of the piece, a human soul in its totality, in its fluctuating action, and in the finest vibrations by which the nerves are thrilled. This drama may not, indeed, be a mere portraiture of character, but yet a development, or rather a self unfolding, of a character face to face with the misery of this world. According to this design of the whole, Shakespeare does not mark single defects, but, painting and adding, he unfolds, partly by action and partly by inaction, the lineaments which combine to form a piquant and original portrait."

The truth often lies between the extremes of interpretation. Hamlet may be conceived as not deficient in ordinary will power, as equal to the exigencies of ordinary affairs, or even more largely endowed. But still the *situation* in which he is placed is beyond *his* powers. Perhaps he is not to be blamed for want of success, which mortals cannot command; but we feel, time and again, that he pronounces his own condemnation, which the circumstances justify, when he trifles with his opportunity.

"Thus conscience does make cowards of us all,
And thus the native hue of resolution
Is sicklied o'er with the pale cast of thought;

> And enterprises of great pith and moment,
> With this regard their currents turn awry,
> And lose the name of action."

This is the explanation of Hamlet's defect and the warning to all like him. And his self-reproaches in Act 2, Scene 2, are echoes of this thought.

> "Oh what a rogue and peasant slave am I," etc. . . .
> "But I am pigeon livered and lack gall
> To make oppression bitter."

One of the surest ways to misread and misinterpret the true spirit and purpose of this play, or of any of Shakespeare's plays, is to presuppose that the Dramatist, the Poet, the Maker, has violated the fundamental law of poetical production. Poetry is creation, not analysis. It is a correlation of spiritual forces with their material forms, resulting in a concrete entity. Science may dissect it, criticism may expound it, but, unless a soul has been breathed into it by the inspiration of genius, it must be "a thing of shreds and patches," a puppet, a skeleton perhaps, but not a living, enduring poem; and in no form of poetry is this more true than in the drama. As Coleridge says of him, "Shakespeare is the Spinozistic deity—an omnipresent creativeness." Shakespeare, of all men, did not plan Moralities, did not dress up abstractions—Virtue, Loyalty, Piety, etc.,—to act a little charade. Had he done so the dust of centuries would have entombed his dramas, along with the Miracle Plays and Moralities of his predecessors. But they live. And why? Because they were born, not made; of poem, as well as of poet, it is true, "*Nascitur, non fit.*"

Shakespeare's persons of the drama are veritable men, not lay figures ; and they are organic men, not mechanical toys—manikins. In each we behold Shakespeare's conception of an individual, often grander, more heroic, in proportions, than the original, because Shakespeare himself was greater. And thus with care we may discover in his portraits the original, plus the hand, the head, the kindly smile, the capacious brain of the artist himself.

Hence, as Hazlitt says, Hamlet is a portrait. Whose portrait he was originally intended for is one thing ; what he became in process of development is another. Far be it from me to deny that in the completed Hamlet who speaks to us from the Second Quarto, who speaks to us from under the vizard of Booth, we hear a voice that is truly Shakespeare's. We do see his veritable likeness there, and our own also. The great dramatist has projected himself into his creation, and taught him to utter the thoughts that shook his own high-wrought soul as it trembled in the balance. This is *one* side of the many-sided man, at a critical juncture of his life, and the speculation and wide discourse that flash from the lips of the melancholy Dane are inspirations such as the Delphic God gave out through the voice of his human oracle.

If we cast aside his inky robes, and consider young Hamlet, not as a prince, but as a man, we discover the secret of his wide and perennial interest for us. The image of the philosophic soul, reflected from the mirror of the poet's mind, stands posed in sweetness and strength, like a demi-god. Before it is the heavy burthen of life, weighted with cares, with conflicting and doubtful duties, with certain peril, and with possible crime. In the shadowy lines of the spirit we behold the intellect perplexed, the conscience appalled, the will paralyzed, and the whole man borne down in a vain struggle with destiny. Equipped from a full armory with every weapon of the intellect, a fatal defect of will mars and ruins all. Is not such a picture, projected from the depths of the poet's nature for the teaching of the world, an open confession as it were, a crying aloud ; "I have sinned?" Here is "that unmatched form and feature of blown youth, blasted with ecstasy," and "quite, quite, down;" "and, in his up-shot, purposes mistook fallen on the inventors' heads." Purpose, decision, prompt and resolute action, this is the lesson for the King, for the Court, for us, for the world, for future generations, and, perhaps, most of all. for the easing of the poet's own heart and conscience.

THE AUTHORSHIP OF HAMLET.

> "Unless my study and my books be false,
> The argument you held was wrong."
> 1 *Henry* VI., I. 1.

IF my interpretation of the Significance of Hamlet seems to any one more like to a cento of others' opinions than to a cast of my own thought, I might plead a goldsmith's apology, who should think his jewel none the worse that it showed more of gems than of setting. But of this excuse I will not avail myself, for, little as I may obtrude my own views, they are the conclusions of a quarter of a century of mingled interested inquiry and unconscious cerebration. My theories of Shakespeare and his works, such as they are, have been fused over the slow fires of a lifetime of admiring contemplation, for I cannot call it real study: and the treasures that I have imbedded in the slag of my essay are there as illustrations—forcible for intrinsic worth, or beautiful for expression—of results obtained through my own examination and independent reflection. So much, I may be permitted by way of apology for my method.

Who wrote Hamlet? Shakespeare, of course! But is it of course? The Baconian theory aside, it is conceded that Shakespeare did write the play, as it is presented to us in the best modern texts, and as it is acted by the most reputable tragedians. But where did the play come from, and how much of it is really Shakespeare's in kernel, as well as in shell? This has seemed to be a hard nut for Shakespearians to crack, and this lecture is designed to show that it is more simple than has been imagined, and that many of the difficulties were rather of men's own making than intrinsic to the subject.

Modern criticism agrees that there were three plays called Hamlet. Our accepted version, which is substantially the same in all the best recent editions, with mere slight verbal deviations and varying constructions, rests upon the volume published in 1623 by the companions of Shakespeare, and known as the First Folio, as verified and modified by reference to the edition authorized by Shakespeare himself, the Second Quarto of 1604, which it probably followed. All the best modern editions may be regarded as containing the genuine Hamlet, and are as nearly Shakespeare's as human research can rehabilitate the thought of three centuries ago. The Second Quarto, on which they finally rest, is distinctively and assuredly genuine. It is not merely Shakespearian, it is Shakespeare's; it is Shakespeare! Let us name it the Last Hamlet.

It is well known how indifferent, if not averse, to the publication of his plays was Shakespeare, as were many other dramatists of his day. It is, however, sufficiently clear why he authorized the publication of Hamlet in 1604 in the form known as the Second Quarto. In 1603 an edition of Hamlet was printed, now known as the First Quarto. The title of this book was: "The tragicall Historie of Hamlet Prince, of Denmarke By William Shakespeare. As it hath beene diuerse times acted by his Highnesse seruants in the Cittie of London : as also in the two Vniuersities of Cambridge and Oxford, and elsewhere." The next year the Second Quarto was published with the following title-page : "The Tragicall Historie of Hamlet, Prince of Denmarke. By William Shakespeare. Newly imprinted and enlarged to almost as much again as it was, according to the true and perfect Coppie," etc., 1604." The two versions vary widely, and there has been much dispute as to why they should so differ, when printed so nearly together, and each purporting to give Shakespeare's play.

There are three theories as to the intrinsic character of Quarto First (Q 1). One theory is that it is merely a mangled copy of the true version as we have it in Quarto Second; and that the discrepancies between them are due to the fact that it was carelessly taken down in short-hand, during the representation, and that the blanks were filled in from memory by an incompetent person, who mutilated and marred it in the reproduction. This view necessarily attributes the authorship to Shakespeare.

A second theory is summed up in the view taken by the Clarendon Editors, and is thus entitled to all the weight mere authority can give, though they admit that it is "conjectural, and based to a large extent on subjective considerations." According to this theory we have in the Second Quarto, for the first time, the Hamlet of Shakespeare. The Clarendon Editors reach this conclusion, although "in the Quarto of 1603 we have the whole 'action' of the play: that is to say, the events follow very much in the same order, and the catastrophe is the same." The following is their view: "we venture to think that a close examination of Quarto First will convince any one that it contains some of Shakespeare's undoubted work, mixed with a great deal that is not his, and will confirm our theory that the text, imperfect as it is, represents an older play in a transition state, while it was undergoing a remodelling, but had not received more than the first rough touches of the great master's hand."

This opinion has been held by many eminent commentators; but, on the other hand, the weight of authority rests with a third theory, that Q 1, though evidently an older and feebler play than the Last Hamlet,—Q 2—, was in fact largely, if not altogether, Shakespeare's work, and gives the play as it was performed before it was recast by the author about 1596, or 1597, and as it now exists.

When the Hamlet of Q 2 took its form, it is not quite easy to say. Singer puts the date at 1597, Malone at 1600. Richard Grant White and Clark and Wright place the date between 1598 and 1602. I prefer the earliest of these dates, or even 1596, as the initial point of the Last Hamlet, though its revision may have lasted till 1603, and, it is not improbable, considering the ways of authors, that even after the pirated First Quarto was published, and when the Second Quarto was in its birth-throes, in 1604, Shakespeare may have welcomed its coming with some rose of poesy, or set therein as a coronal for the newcome Prince, Scotch James, or Hamlet the Perennial, some of the jewels we prize the most.

"In 1597 the Lord Admiral's players were restrained for a time from playing, in consequence of having brought out Nash's Isle of Dogs, a play in which personal satire was probably introduced, and for which the author was imprisoned." (Hamlet, Clar. Ed. Preface). Nothing is said of "Innovation," or "Inhibition," in Q 1, which contains the old cast of Hamlet; but Q 2 has in regard to the Gonzago players, "I think their inhibition comes by the means of the late innovation." This is not without significance as to the point of time when the recast of the play was made; for if the Inhibition was but just issued when Shakespeare was rewriting Hamlet, nothing could be more natural than an allusion to it as a matter of deepest interest to actors and playgoers.

The Second Quarto is declared to be a "true and perfect copy," "newly imprinted and enlarged to almost as much again as it was." The First Quarto, on the other hand, only claims to be an actor's copy, "Hamlet," "as it has been divers times acted by his Highness' servants," etc. These phrases probably express the true distinction between them. There was no wish, or inclination, on the part of the Company of The King's Players, to which Shakespeare belonged, to publish its plays, the repertory of which, while it remained exclusively its own, constituted a valuable stock-in-trade. But, it is probable that in 1603 there was a lively public interest in the popular play of Hamlet, and, to profit by this, an "enterprising" publisher, one "N. L.," procured and put upon the market an actor's copy, probably an imperfect one that had been cast aside—likely enough, one that had been used at one of the Universities mentioned in the imprint, and which had fallen into "innocuous desuetude." But in the meantime, the great dramatist had rewritten and expanded this play which had formerly held the stage, and which neither he, nor his company, was now willing to acknowledge as the full-grown child of his genius. He does not repudiate the First Qnarto, as not his work, in the imprint of Q 2, but suggests its imperfections, its incorrectness and its obsolete form. Quarto Second was issued from a correct copy of this new cast of the play, though it was printed with the customary carelessness of the age.

The discrepancies between the two forms of the play are too marked to permit the supposition that the one is a mere mutilation of the other; and, inferior as Q 1 is to Q 2, it is too consistent, and too good an acting play as it stands, to be accepted as a mere fragment. To my mind Q 2 exhibits change, process and development from Q 1; and in conception as well as in form. It contains three thousand seven hundred and nineteen lines, while Q 1 numbers only two thousand one hundred and forty three lines, nearly verifying the statement of the imprint, that it had been enlarged to almost as much again. The language differs widely, the order of scenes is not the same, and even the names of persons of the drama are changed. In Q 1, Polonius is Corambis; Reynaldo, Montano ; Osric, "a braggart gentleman ; " and there are other minor variations in the names. But the play itself is substantially and essentially the same ; "all the *action* of the amended Hamlet is to be found in the first sketch ; " and this is a very essential point.

The First Quarto had independent merits of its own, sufficient, indeed, to commend it to a certain class of minds as the better form of stage play even, and it has served as the basis of such plays in Germany. This, however, is chiefly due to its brevity and greater rapidity of action. In it the actual madness of Hamlet appears more probable, while in Q. 2 the language that might lead us to believe that madness real is modified. So the guilt of the Queen is more emphasized in Q 2 ; and other points of difference might be noted.

Knight well says : "The character of Hamlet is fully conceived in the original play, whenever he is in action. It is the contemplative part of his nature which is elaborated in the perfect copy." The greatest and most radical change from the earliert to the later tragedy, however, is in the infusion of a loftier tone of thought. The former was a drama of plot and situations ; but the speculative reason of Shakespeare has breathed into the mature Hamlet his own spirit, which finds play in its noblest passages. Much more might be said, but the main point is that the earlier play served only as the stalk and bud for the great tragedy, and that in the full blown Hamlet we have the flower of Shakespeare's admirable judgment and ripe imagination.

I have said there were three Hamlets. The last Hamlet, that of Q 2, undoubtedly Shakespeare's, which substantially took its present cast about 1597; the earlier Hamlet of Q 1, in parts questionably Shakespeare's, according to some critics; and another, or the First Hamlet. My theory of Q 1 is that it was a stage copy of the earlier version, and was probably dropped from the stage by Shakespeare's Company, in or before, 1596, or possibly on account of the Inhibition in 1597; although it may have been produced by amateurs elsewhere, "at the Universities," later. It was printed for the first time in 1603, and, crude as it appears to us, must present the drama after it had been considerably developed from its original rudimentary form, by accretions, suggestions and amendments.

Corrupt as is the text, and inferior as Q. 1 may seem to some, it evinces in every part the essential features of a Shakespearian creation. The only doubt of this is based upon intrinsic evidence of very shadowy texture. But at all events it is the earliest form of the play remaining to us. The earliest draft of the tragedy—the First Hamlet—is a hypothetical play, of which no copy exists, and which we cannot certainly prove was at all different from Q 1, but which may be assumed to have existed, and which might well be entitled, "Hamlet, Revenge!", as it was mockingly called by Shakespeare's satirists.

We have now traced this play backward to its earliest verified form. Writers generally agree that an inceptive play, or original cast of a play, called Hamlet, did exist, and was acted as early as 1589, or fourteen years before Q 1 was printed. As to whether this is the play we have in Q 1, or not, there has been discussion. If not contained in Q 1, it is no longer extant. We have no certain proof that Q 1 does not contain this original cast of Hamlet, but the circumstances lead to a contrary belief, and to the view that it is much developed from the first sketch. Fleay says, Hamlet is "Founded on an older play now lost."

It has been generally assumed, or admitted without question, that this original play was not composed by Shakespeare, but by some one else, though some of the most learned and careful of his editors see no ground for such an opinion. While these lectures may add little that is really new to the knowledge of a subject which has been so thoroughly examined by patient scholarship, and while no absolute demonstration can be made of any theory of it without the discovery of additional evidence, yet it is hoped that the facts herein presented will at least throw upon the genesis and evolution of this drama a light strong and clear enough to exhibit who was its original author, and when, how, and why, it was written.

And if it should turn out that my contention in the matter is right, and that William Shakespeare was the builder of Hamlet from the bottom up, my hearers may conclude that the upshot is much like "the Dutch taking Holland." But then again it is something if we can prove once in a while that things *are* what they seem, and that to the common-sense of mankind is occasionally accorded a clearer vision of the truth than to the combined green-goggles and strabismus of literary thaumaturgists.

There is diversity of opinion as to who wrote the original play. Usually, the burden of proof would rest upon those who deny the first conception of a play to its author; here this rule of evidence has been reversed, and it is assumed that Shakespeare did not originate Hamlet. Halliwell, whose opinion, as such, is entitled to the greatest deference, sums up one theory as follows in his "Dictionary of Old Plays." He cites: "Hamlet. A play with this title acted at Newington Theatre by the Lord Admiral's and Lord Chamberlain's men, June 9th, 1594. It *preceded* Shakespeare's tragedy, and is several times alluded to by contemporary writers."

This statement takes for granted the point at issue, but it rests solely upon conjecture, and no extrinsic evidence is offered to prove who was the author. Now, as has been said, either Q 1 represents the earliest draft of Hamlet, or, as is more generally believed, there was a still ruder version in possession of the stage for many years, as stated by Halliwell. If the former supposition be true, whoever else had a hand in it, it was, to all intents and purposes, Shakespeare's. If the latter, we shall have to consider what other tragic author so well satisfies the conditions required for its production. To my mind the evidence appears conclusive that the same hand laid the foundation that placed the capstone upon this admirable literary edifice. As I have said before, the burden of proof rests upon those who deny its authorship to the man whom contemporary opinion, with no glimmer of a doubt, assigned it to. Let us review the evidence.

The Clarendon Editors hold that the internal evidence shows that Q 1 was inadequate to the genius of Shakespeare. Much more so would be a lamer, ruder, version of the play. In 1597 he was, indeed, capable of greater things—of the greatest,—for it was then that he wrote the last Hamlet; but ten years earlier, when it was first hatched, his was a fledgling's wing, and not the flight of the eagle. But even then it would be difficult to point to any one in 1587, or 1588, capable of producing it, except Shakespeare himself, or perhaps Marlowe. Hence Fleay (Shakespeare Manual, p. 41) says, "I have little doubt that the early Hamlet of 1589 was written by Shakespeare and Marlowe in conjunction, and that portions of it can be traced in Quarto First, as Corambis Hamlet."

On the other hand, much of the argument by other advocates of a prae-Shakespearian play is directed against Shakespeare's ability in 1589, aged 25—much less in 1585, aged 21,—to produce even a rough draft of Hamlet, or indeed any sketch at all for the stage. Whatever may be the weight of either argument, they do not consist. They are mutally destructive; and, indeed, the truth probably lies between the extremes. Shakespeare at 21 could not have produced the Hamlet we have, to which these critics evidently revert, but he was quite adequate to the original play, and better able to write it than any other man. It would seem that those who deny to Shakespeare the authorship of the original draft of Hamlet should suggest who else did, or could, compose it. If it were a work of genius, and even the germ of Hamlet must have had merit, who besides Shakespeare, or Marlowe, could have written it? If it were crude, or rude, with the mere potentialities of its supreme excellence, why could not the same man originate it, who subsequently developed it? Is not any other conjecture mere guesswork, or a mythopoic process?

Timmins, in his preface to the Devonshire Hamlets, says, "My conviction is that in Q 1 we have a 'rough hewn' draft of a noble drama, (written probably in 1587–1589). Fleay also puts the first Hamlet in 1589. Some writers place its date even earlier, and Furness, with all the lights before him, fixes on 1585-6. But we can safely say that it must have been written before 1589—as early as 1588—to call forth the satirical allusions to it, written by rival authors in 1589, which recognized it as a well known play then; and, there can be scarcely a doubt that it must have appeared in the previous year, 1587, or even in 1586, to have come into public notice and favor by 1589.

The following incidental opinion from one of the more brilliant critics of Shakespeare has its value.

"Thus, since, he certainly possessed a share in the theatre, in 1589, we may well credit the account of the performances, in that very year, of his Hamlet; that is, as it was first played, wanting its present grander poetry and passion. We have no vestige of Hamlet in its first state; but if it was not superior to his Romeo and Juliet, before that tragedy was rewritten, there is not the slightest difficulty in supposing it was one of his first dramatic attempts."

(Chas. Armitage Brown in "Shakespeare's Autobiographical Poems," p. 28).

Chas. Knight, who cannot be too much commended for the spirit in which he edited Shakespeare and the methods he employed, says:

"Not a tittle of evidence exists to show that there was any play of Hamlet but that of Shakespeare; and all the collateral evidence upon which it is inferred that an earlier play of Hamlet than Shakespeare's did exist, may, on the other hand, be taken to prove that Shakespeare's sketch was in repute at an earlier period than is commonly assigned to its date." He concludes that "the Taming of the Shrew and Hamlet were both very early productions of Shakespeare." There is scarcely a doubt that Romeo and Juliet belongs to the same period. Knight's view is held substantially by a number of the ablest commentators on Shakespeare, though they differ in details; among others, Delius, Elze, Staunton, and Gervinus.

To my mind the strongest argument against Shakespeare's authorship of the earlier play is the dictum of the Clarendon Editors, whom I have always found it unwise hastily to disagree with. In philological questions and the decision of disputed interpretations, they evince a skill and critical faculty rarely at fault. Indeed, if they had not assigned their reasons for it, their decision, usually so judicious, would be almost conclusive with me. But when they allege, "a complete absence of positive evidence," "for Shakespeare's connection with the play before 1602," they go too far. They all quote, as "strong negative evidence", the omission of Hamlet from a list of

Shakespeare's plays made by Francis Meres in 1598. But this is a *non sequitur*, as other of his plays were omitted in the list, and plays which are doubtful were included in it, as Titus Andronicus and Love's Labor's Won. But, to save the point of the omission, the Clarendon Editors exclude from the catalogue of Shakespeare's plays, Pericles and Henry VI, which are not mentioned in Meres' list.

The whole value of Meres' List, as evidence, may be summed up as follows. Francis Meres, a scholarly and competent writer, in his "Wits' Treasury," in 1598, gives the first direct notice of Shakespeare's works, naming twelve of his plays, among which Hamlet is not mentioned. He places Shakespeare, as a poet, with Homer, Virgil and Ovid and the Greek Tragedians, and with Sidney, Spenser, Daniel, Drayton, Warner, Marlowe and Chapman, the most admired poets of his own age. He adds, "As Plautus and Seneca are accounted the best for Comedy and Tragedy among the Latins, so Shakespeare among the English is the most excellent in both kinds for the stage: for comedy, *witness* his Gentlemen of Verona, his Errors, his Love's Labor's Lost, his Love's Labor's Won, his Midsummer Night's Dream, and his Merchant of Venice; for tragedy, his Richard II, Richard III, Henry IV, King John, Titus Andronicus, and his Romeo and Juliet." Identifying Love's Labor's Won as All's Well that Ends Well, are we to treat this as an accurate and exhaustive list of plays which had then been produced by Shakespeare? It is almost certain that Henry VI (lst part), Pericles, The Taming of the Shrew, and probably Much Ado about Nothing were in existence when Meres printed his book. Nor does it seem to have been the intention of Meres to give this as a full list of Shakespeare's plays, else why does he employ this word "witness," which seems to imply that his purpose was merely to cite his favorite plays, or those then most in vogue? And it might well be that the early plays not mentioned by him had, after a more or less successful career upon the stage, fallen into temporary neglect. Indeed, it might be conjectured that such partial eclipse induced Shakespeare to withdraw Hamlet from the stage for final study and revision about this time, which gave us his mature Hamlet, as we now have it, though I beg that no one will consider me as attaching undue importance to such mere conjectures. But it may have influenced him, as the Inhibition may likewise have weighed with him, and the death of his son, and domestic sorrows, and personal discontents, and most of all the fullness of literary inspiration and its urgency and solicitings. I think, however, it will be admitted as significant that Meres does not mention Pericles, Henry VI, or the Taming of the Shrew, which without doubt had enjoyed popularity and were at least attributed to Shakespeare. And it is worth noting, too, that, at the date of Meres' publication, 1598, Shakespeare's greatest plays had not been yet produced. For some reason that epoch opened to him the portals of a new spiritual life, and a new line of dramatic creation. Othello, Macbeth, Lear, Cymbeline, the Tempest, and many others, on which his reputation chiefly rests, followed his Last Hamlet. Thus, then, though the secondary plays of Shakespeare placed him, at thirty-four years of age, in the estimation of Meres and his contemporaries, with the greatest poets, and above all those who are held out to us as possible authors of Hamlet, we are asked to believe that, at twenty-three or twenty-four years of age, he lacked the invention to adapt an old legend to the stage, and had to depend upon some forerunner, who never otherwise evinced any capacity for great works, for help to lay out for him the ground plan of the play. It is Meres, too, who says, " that the Muses would speak with Shakespeare's fine filed phrase, if they would speak English," which I commend to those who have argued his personality away, or who portray him as a phantom or a fraud or an ignoramus.

Malone (in 1821) says, "*Perhaps* the original Hamlet was written by Thomas Kyd, who was the author of one play, (and probably of more) to which no name is affixed. In Kyd's Spanish Tragedy, as in Shakespeare's Hamlet, there is, if I may say so, a play represented within a play ; if the old play of Hamlet should ever be recovered, a similar interlude, I make no doubt, would be found there," etc. But what of it? How does it matter? There is nothing in this sort of criticism. The same device will be frequently found in the annals of the stage, as in the "Rehearsal." But facts appear, which are indeed curious, if we remember that Malone's hypothesis has been passed along from one commentator and historian to another almost unquestioned.

Skottowe and Collier, in turn, speak of "the old play of Hamlet," as antecedent to Shakespeare's, as if of course, but offer no proof. Lowndes, in his "Bibliographer's Manual," mentions "Kyd's old play of Hamlet." Dyce thinks that the First Hamlet "might have been written by Kyd." All this proceeds upon the hypothesis that Shakespeare was a mere adapter of other man's plays, and could make none of his own—an entirely groundless assumption.

Mr. Fleay puts down the Spanish Tragedy as probably written before, 1589, though not published until 1594. Symonds, in "Shakespeare's Predecessors" (page 486), describing "the Tragedy of Blood," as he calls it, says, "Thomas Kyd—*if* Hieronymo and the Spanish Tragedy are correctly ascribed to him—may be called the founder of this species. About his life we know absolutely nothing, although it may be plausibly conjectured that he received a fair academical education." Thus Hamlet is to be attributed to Kyd, about whom this able literary historian knows nothing, because of a supposed analogy to the Spanish Tragedy, the authorship of which is doubtful. And why? Because each is a Tragedy of Blood, and has a play within a play. But this is rather a reason for assigning the foundling "Spanish Tragedy" to Shakespeare than Hamlet to Kyd. Here is one play of uncertain paternity with an interlude in it; but almost all of Shakespeare's earliest plays have something of the sort; *argal*, Kyd wrote Hamlet!

Passing by the Gonzago Play in Hamlet, we find the Taming of the Shrew tacked on to an induction, and played before the famous Christopher Sly. It was produced about 1589, and Hamlet the same year, or earlier, as Fleay tells us, and as is probable.

Midsummer Night's Dream, written in 1592, if not earlier, has its play within a play—a most worshipful interlude; and Love's Labor's Lost has a masque, in which rustic actors come in to be derided by the lords and ladies. The play within a play was a natural theatrical device at a period when the most favored part of the audience occupied seats on the stage, a survival of which appears in our modern fashionable and inconvenient proscenium boxes. It belonged, too, to a period of the utmost confusion in literary forms, when an ingenious combination of several plots was a frequent and favorite resort of the playwrights. The Masque was used constantly by Marston, Webster and Tourneur in their Tragedies; and Greene has an Induction to his James IV., in which Oberon, King of the Fairies, has the chief part. The play within a play was a relic among the traditions of the stage, and Shakespeare, or the manager under whom he wrote, retained it in his earlier dramas; but his true artistic instinct soon disembarrassed itself from an artifice more or less clumsy, and which lost its theatrical propriety as the drama assumed the form with which Shakespeare himself chiefly stamped it.

Halliwell says in his edition of Karl Simrock's Remarks, in regard to the ascription of the earliest Hamlet to Thomas Kyd: "This is mere conjecture. If, as is most probable, an older play on the subject of Hamlet existed at the time when Shakespeare wrote his tragedy, we have no evidence whatever that will lead us to believe that it was written by Kyd."

Here the case stands. No proof is adduced for the

authorship of Kyd, who has been generally assumed to be the writer of the First Hamlet; and for Marlowe's greater, or lesser, share in its composition, we have only such evidence as may be drawn from the conclusion that he had an abler and more forceful genius than Shakespeare. It is not difficult to sympathize with the enthusiasm which seeks to rescue from an unmerited oblivion a genius like Marlowe's, and to rehabilitate it in the empire of thought. But his own proper niche must be assigned to each, and every statue must stand upon its own pedestal. We must not rob, or borrow, one shred of reputation from any other to deck him whom we would honor. Marlowe's fame must depend on Faustus, the Jew of Malta, and Edward II, and we can gain nothing by claiming for him without proof, the title to Hamlet.

The whole theory of a prae-Shakespearian Hamlet proceeds upon the supposition that Shakespeare could not write it, but that somebody else could. Who was this somebody? Why should Kyd, or even mighty Marlowe, be summoned from oblivion to sit as teachers to him who cast them all into the darkest shade? This is not the way we reason about other matters. Plots, it is true, were then common property. No rule of courtesy forbade the use by one writer, or many, of the same plot or theme employed by other authors. Collaboration was common enough; but, when we are shown any other tragedy approaching Shakespeare's, we may concede the point that he needed a teacher to coach him in tragedy-making at twenty-five, or even at twenty-one, years of age.

Curiously enough, out of all the swarm of play-writers of his era, Shakespeare is not only the greatest tragedian, but the only dramatist whose tragedies hold the English stage with an unceasing, never-fatiguing interest. We find sweet and noble poetry, powerful situations and other merits enshrined in the forgotten dramas of others, but they remain now merely as stately monuments. Occasionally some tragedy by another is revived for the personal behoof of a "Star," who thinks it fitted to his personal qualities, but it soon passes beneath the horizon, and only Hamlet, Othello, Lear, and Macbeth remain, shining on continually, like the constellations that cluster around the Polar Star.

Two bands of destructives are at work on Shakespeare. I trust they will not deem me discourteous, for I respect their motives, when I style them literary wreckers. One would transfer his entire literary estate in the lump to the rich heritage of the late Lord Bacon; the other is sedulously striving to distribute his dramatic effects and fame among the poverty-stricken ghosts of his contemporaries. In his own day, and for nearly two hundred years thereafter, nobody else was even hinted at as having so much as dipped his finger into Hamlet. But a pedant dropped an *ovum* of alien authorship, and it hatched to a bee in his bonnet; and now a swarm that have sucked the honey of Shakespeare's flowers are for hiving it in other men's waxen cells. One play they give, on the strength of the internal evidences, to some unknown or forgotten writer; another, to some other; until, in this parting of his vestments, the great dramatist is left in rags and almost naked. What we need is some honest Shakespearian who will take the time, toil and trouble to wipe out the baseless fabric of these "internal evidences" that evince nothing.

It will scarcely be denied that *somebody* wrote Hamlet as early as 1589, or earlier. Elze adduces as a bit of circumstantial evidence for a much earlier production of the play, and its Shakespearian authorship, the following facts : first, that Euphuism is ridiculed in the scenes with Osric and with the Gravedigger. He tells us that, in the scene with the latter, Hamlet alludes to the "three years" since the "age has grown so picked." Lyly's Euphues was published in 1581—possibly in 1579; so that 1585 would approximate the term for it to become the vogue. And he ingeniously concludes that this marks the birth of the play. Again, in 1585, Shakespeare's son Hamnet was born, and within a year Shakespeare is believed to have left Stratford and sought his fortunes in London, at the age of twenty-two. Elze pointedly adds, "Is it not readily conceivable that at the very beginning of his career he should have chosen a subject for his pen which bore the same name as his beloved boy, and that he should have recurred to it afterwards with undisguised preference? Hamnet died in 1596; and this blow must have fallen most heavily on the father, may possibly have led him to take up once more this spiritual child of the same name. Who can estimate the effect which grief for his only son may not have had in producing that deep-seated melancholy and distaste for the vanity of the world which have found in this tragedy their immortal expression? This view is emphasized by the philosophical and passionate speculation of Hamlet, in the second or complete play, but not in the earlier draft of it." Hamlet, or Hamnet, was a not uncommon forename in that day and in the vicinity of Stratford, and Hamnet is also found as a surname thereabouts.

The earliest allusion to Hamlet is by Nash in an Epistle prefixed to Greene's Menaphon, printed in 1589, and possibly in 1587, as there is some ground for believing, and reads as follows: "It is a common practice now a daies amongst a sort of shifting companions, that runne through every arte and thrive by none, to leave the trade of Noverint whereto they were borne, and busie themselves with the indevours of arte, that could scarcelie latinize their necke-verse if they should have neede; yet English Seneca read by candlelight yeeldes manie good sentences, as 'Blould as a beggar,' and so forth; and if you intreate him faire in a frostie morning, he will afford you whole Hamlets, I should say Handfulls, of tragical speaches."

Fleay, a recent writer of great industry, research and ingenuity, asserts that Simpson had demonstrated that this only refers to Shakespeare as an *actor*, and hence that this passage has no reference to his authorship of Hamlet. To me it seems that "to latinize their neck verse," i.e., to put into Latin a verse from the Psalms so as to give them "benefit of the clergy," and by this text save their necks from the gallows, was rather the function of a writer than of a play-actor, who has no need of Latin now, and had none then; and the reading of an English, or translated, Seneca, for quotation, paraphrase, or plagiary, was in like manner work for the closet and not for the stage. Moreover, it is well-nigh certain that Shakespeare never played leading parts, or won much distinction as an actor, and that he had acquired considerable means within four years after he arrived in London. He could not have made much money as an actor, hence we must infer that it was as a writer, and shareholder in his company. But, whoever the author may be, the quotation from Nash shows that there was a play of Hamlet, written by somebody who is styled a 'Noverint,' as early as 1589, at least. We shall discuss later whether this Noverint was Shakespeare, but it may be said here that Lord Campbell's small book on "Shakespeare's Legal Acquirements," leaves little doubt that he was in early life a Noverint, or attorney's clerk.

A Boston gentleman, Mr. Franklin Fisk Heard, has also produced an agreeable and well-considered little book on "Shakespeare as a Lawyer," which fortifies this view.

But these references, as allusions to Shakespeare, received confirmation some years later, 1592, in the slurs of Greene, who had grown more and more embittered against this "Johannes Factotum," "this Shakescene"; a versatile Jack-of-all-trades, who wrote, doubtless, in many manners, tragedy, comedy, history, and likewise acted in his own dramas, and who had on hand a poem, "Venus and Adonis", that won for him the patronage of the young Maecenas of Southampton.

This wretched Greene, in his Groatsworth of Wit, published in 1592, uses language, which cannot refer to any other than Shakespeare, as the play upon his name evinces, as well as the reference to a line in Henry VI, Part 3, "O tiger's heart, wrapt in a woman's hide." He says,

"An upstart crow beautified * with our feathers that, with his
'Tiger's heart, wrapt in a player's hide ',"
supposes he is as well able to bombast out a blank verse as the best of you, and, being an absolute Johannes Factotum, is in his own conceit the only Shakescene in a country, etc." Stress has been laid upon the fact that Greene assails him here as 'a player': but, if such be the fact, still player and playwright were almost synonyms at that day, so the distinction goes for nothing; and the language applies as well to the one as the other.

Chettle, in his Kind Hart's Dream, 1592, thus apologizes for, or repudiates, the foregoing:

"About three months since died Mr. Robert Greene, leaving many papers in sundry booksellers' hands, among others his Groatsworth of Wit, in which a letter written to divers playwriters is offensively by one or two of them taken: and because on the dead they cannot be avenged, they wilfully forge in their conceits a living author; and after tossing it to and fro, no remedy but it must needs light on me .... With neither of them that take offense was I acquainted, and with one of them

* "Beautified is a vile phrase." Was this introduced in reply to Greene? Hamlet, Clarendon. Act 2, S. 2, v. III.

(Marlowe?) I care not if I never be. The other (Shakespeare?) whom at that time I did not so much spare as since I wish I had . . . . that I did not I am as sorry as if the original fault had been my fault; because myself have seen his demeanor no less civil than he excellent in the quality he professes. Besides, divers of worship have reported his uprightness of dealing, which argues his honesty; and his facetious grace in writing, that approves his art . . . . I protest it was all Greene's, and not mine nor Master Nash's, as some have unjustly affirmed."

The significance of these attacks by the envious and dissolute Nash, and the gifted, but profligate, Greene, will be apparent, when we remember that they belonged to a rival band of dramatic authors, and attributed their literary failures to the malign influence of the company of players in which Shakespeare had become the most important writer. We know from Henslow's Diary (p. 8) that Hamlet continued to hold the stage, and was acted June 9th, 1594, by a company of players, to which Shakespeare belonged. Lodge, in 1596, refers to it (p. 9), when he mentioned, "Ye ghost which cried so miserally (sic) at ye theator, like an oisterwife, *Hamlet, Revenge!*"

Permit me now to call your attention to the following points. The First Hamlet was played in or before 1589; probably two or three years earlier. In 1589, it was ascribed to a Noverint, or attorney's clerk. Competent persons, learned in the law, discover in the undoubted work of Shakespeare evidences, very weighty if not entirely conclusive, that he was well equipped with legal phraseology, full of it, and in his earliest writings quite saturated with it. The allusions of his rivals a little later seem to fix upon him a connection with this play of Hamlet, so that, in default of a claimant even to this *nom de plume* of Noverint, we must leave the holder in possession. All the positive evidence is in favor of Shakespeare's authorship: popular opinion, competent contemporaneous witnesses, his own unquestioned ownership, a *quasi*-copyright, the admissions of his enemies, and the claims of his friends, colleagues and posthumous publishers. The attempt to parcel out the plays of Shakespeare among the dramatists of his day is a failure, because there is no testimony to lead to such a conclusion. The dividers of the spoil cannot agree among themselves as to who is entitled to share in it, and the beggars they would clothe in the purple betray their personality in every phase of their mock royalty. The only evidence cited against this view is of that filmy and esoteric character which depends on the intuitions of critics as to style, or on its conformity to certain arbitrary rules of another school, which are continually found at fault and misleading. More or less value may be attached to Elze's opinions on the coincidence in names and dates of the birth and death of Shakespeare's son, with the inception and revision of this tragedy. The omission from Meres' list could not be passed over, because so much has been made of it by diligent commentators, but when examined without prejudice, it seems too slender a thread to hang a theory on.

It may, in view of all the facts, be affirmed that all the positive and extrinsic evidence is in favor of Shakespeare's authorship of the original Hamlet, while the belief that anybody else wrote it, or had any special share in, or claim to, its production, rests upon mere hypothesis. To accept it, we must admit that Shakespeare was not only phenomenal, but abnormal, and by some miracle was suddenly transformed from a reprobate call-boy to the imperial ruler of thought and imagination. I do not deny that as extraordinary instances may be produced of the rise of men as of their reverses, often independent of merit, where opportunity has played henchman to ability, and greatness has been thrust upon fortune's favorites. But the empire of the mind, unlike success in temporal matters, is above these caprices. It must withstand and survive every assault that can be made, and hence must rest upon reality. Shakespeare's supremacy remains, because what he has said was better said, and better, than other men's utterances.

The certitude of Shakespeare's authorship of Hamlet, *ab ovo*, rests chiefly, after all, in default of disproof, on his undisputed title for so long a time and on the transcendent ability of the man. And if this discussion has no other value it would seem not fruitless, if it brings home to us the great fact of the immense difference in the natural endowments of men—a fact which all the radical and levelling influences of the age are tending to disparage or deny. It is a difference measured by the abyss betwixt imbecility and genius. It has been the fashion of late to confound genius with plodding industry ; as it was formerly, with a spasmodic and eccentric vivacity of fancy. Both conceptions are entirely erroneous. Genius belongs to him who has been lifted up by nature, and is the gift which, because of this higher point of view, confers a wider horizon, a clearer vision, and a deeper insight. Energy is a crucial test of genius, as well as its motive power. No endowments merit the name, or mean the thing, unless they are accompanied by an energy so irresistible that it will not accept denial or defeat in its inquiry and effort for loftier altitudes of life and thought. Energy is an essential constituent of genius ; is its very symbol. On the other hand, mere nervous irritability of intellect, play of fancy, and gushes of eloquence are but the fragments of imagination and reason, and have to be brought into organic unity, and held in well ordered process, in order to be classed with the phenomena of genius even. Sanity, like energy, is a final test of genius. Shakespeare's possession of the sanity and energy of genius establishes the verity of his endowments.

The arguments that would deny to Shakespeare the authorship of the First Hamlet and his other early plays depend upon the theory of mediocrity as a universal fact. All that is required to give assurance that he could take a story as he found it, inform it with his own personality and make of it an immortal play, is to pre-suppose that he had this gift of genius as I have described it.

That this young man from his first appearance in

London exhibited all the criteria of genius is evident from the little we know of his life. Those who only looked to the ease with which he wrote and to the outward form of his plays, but not to the inner light that fills them, spoke of him as an untutored child of nature. Milton, trained in all the knowledge of the schools, says,

> "Sweetest Shakespeare, Fancy's child,
> Warbled his native woodnotes wild,"

and this has been the common view of him. But he was more than this.

His whole career is one of the noblest testimonies on record to the sanity of genius. From the first he set himself to master that organ of expression, language, which was to utter his tuneful thought, be it in sonnet, poem or play. His habits and life were so governed as to enable him to achieve that independence which should place him above "the oppressor's wrong, the proud man's contumely." He evinced an immense ability to labor, and an irresistible impulse for literary creation—the embodiment of thought. His toil was upward; aspiration winged his sandals, and imagination grew the pinions that lifted him above his peers and his successors. We know that Shakespeare wrote the last Hamlet, we are sure that he wrote the second, and who but he could have written the very first Hamlet?

THE EVOLUTION OF HAMLET.

> "As this temple waxes,
> The inward service of the mind and soul
> Grows wide withal....."
> *Hamlet*, I. 3.

In the last lecture I endeavored to show "Who wrote Hamlet," and offered some proofs that not only the last, or completed, Hamlet, was Shakespeare's, but that the very earliest, or hypothetical, Hamlet, also originated with him. I shall now proceed to fortify this view by additional arguments showing the utter improbability that it was the production of any of his contemporaries, together with some further proofs that Shakespeare himself wrote it. My purpose is then to exhibit the manner in which it was developed from a rough sketch to the world-renowned tragedy, together with the subtle influences which perhaps called up from the poet's heart its wonderful soliloquies.

We are too prone to overlook the fact that Shakespeare was not only the greatest dramatist of his own, or any other age, but that he was the founder and creator of the romantic drama as we have it. Nearly all the greater dramatists of that period were the successors of Shakespeare, and, indeed, his disciples. The exception was the group that composed the so-called "University wits," who have been supposed to constitute a rival school of the prophets: Peele, Greene, Nash, Lodge, and Marlowe, to whom may be added, Lyly and Kyd. But Fleay throws great doubt upon their alleged association, if he does not disprove it, and makes a plausible showing for friendship and collaboration between Marlowe and Shakespeare.

In view of Shakespeare's wonderfully genial nature, and his victory over the prejudices of all who came into actual contact with him, it seems not improbable that this surmise of Fleay may have a basis of solid fact. Too much weight, perhaps, should not be laid, however, upon his generous allusion in "As You Like It" to Marlowe, after his wretched and untimely end:

> "Dead Shepherd, now I find thy saw of might:
> 'Who ever loved that loved not at first sight.'"

the second line being quoted from Marlowe's Hero and Leander.

Flashes of wit, bursts of eloquence, flights of poetry and erratic glimpses of dramatic truth abound in the writings of the brilliant band of Bohemians just named; but none of their plays still hold the stage, and to but one of them can be accorded eminent genius. Christopher Marlowe, in his brief and ill-regulated career, evinced powers, which, if matured and chastened, might have added a star of the first magnitude to English Literature; but still he is as much inferior to Shakspeare as he is superior to the boon companions, who, with their phosphorescence, lighted him the way to dusty death. It is generally assumed that Shakespeare is indebted to Marlowe, or others of this crew of rival writers, or to certain (or uncertain) other obscure and unknown playwrights, who are conjectured to have prepared the way for the great dramatist, by providing him with the rough drafts of his dramas, while he merely adapted such outline plays to the stage. An ingenious guess as to such an origin, say of the First Hamlet, is assumed as a basis of argument; and from this postulate is drawn a series of inferences, which are passed on as sober statements, and are finally handed down as historic facts. The evidence for such a concatenation is entirely hypothetical, drawn from the inner consciousness of commentators, and to me seems as baseless and apocryphal as the Bacon-myth matter, (or no matter), and fit only for dismissal to limbo. These phantom dramatists, conjured from oblivion, never appear in any better light than as shadows of the coming poet. The oldest of the so-called University group, Lyly, was only about ten years the senior of Shakespeare; and, according to Fleay, only two of Lyly's and one of Peele's plays were published before Shakespeare's arrival in London, and most of the work of the entire group was done between that date and 1594, when Shakespeare had already become rich and famous. Marlowe's plays, too, were written about the same time with Shakespeare's earlier efforts; so that Shakespeare's dramatic competitors were more strictly his contemporaries than his predecessors.

On one ground or another, often very slight, it is assumed that these literary adventurers all began to produce plays as soon as they came to London, and exhausted themselves by 1592 or 1593; but that Shakespeare, not only the greatest, but the most successful, of them all, was sterile until they had finished their careers, when he burst into a sudden fecundity, and in about ten or twelve years produced his galaxy of dramas. The whole theory is, to my mind, irrational and preposterous. Why should Shakespeare alone be assumed to have been idle, or incompetent, because the barren records of the time do not furnish specifically the dates of his productions, when this is true of all the rest of the dramatists of that period.

Marlowe, the greatest of his competitors, was only three months older than Shakespeare, and came to London about the same time as Shakespeare, or after him. Very little is known of him, and that little, sadly enough, is the story of neglected opportunities, wasted gifts and a blasted life; nevertheless, he has been styled, "The Father of English dramatic poetry." Though the language is too strong, yet it may be fairly conceded that in his hands blank verse first acquired a dignity and power that gave a new meaning to the language of the drama. Symonds assigns the production of his first tragedy, "Tamburlaine," to 1587, when he was but twenty-three years of age; and Bullen, in his Life of Marlowe, concluded that Tamburlaine "had been presented on the stage in, or before, 1588, probably 1587." Why, *à priori*, could not Shakespeare have written the First Hamlet at twenty-three, as well as Marlowe, Tamburlaine? There is not more proof that Marlowe wrote Tamburlaine than that Shakespeare wrote the first Hamlet; indeed, Malone inferred, on poor data it is true, that Tamburlaine was written by Nash. I am not inclined to give more than due weight to tradition, but uncontradicted contemporary opinion is certainly of more value than paradoxical doubts of the same, resting often on shadowy surmises. Why should not Marlowe's Tamburlaine have been written by Marlowe, and Kyd's Spanish Tragedy by Kyd, and Shakespeare's Hamlet by Shakespeare? The popular voice and the belief of intimate friends and hostile critics took it for granted in their own day and generation, and we have no other evidence so good. It is no disparagement to Shakespeare to say that Marlowe was of a more precocious genius, that he came to London better prepared by education for a successful career, and that his reputation was won earlier. But to treat Shakespeare as a scholar, follower, or imitator, of Marlowe, is fanciful. They were contemporaries, and, starting together in the flight for fame, rose with well-matched strength till Marlowe fell, while Shakespeare's transcendent pinion mounted and bore him on to the empyrean.

The lives of all these men are quite as obscure as Shakespeare's early history. We may agree with Halliwell who says, (Outlines, 8th ed. Vol. 1, p. 95), "There is not, indeed, a single particle of evidence respecting his career during the next five years, that is to say, from the Lambert negotiation in 1587, until he is discovered as a rising actor and dramatist in 1592:" and the same may be said of his rivals, but this only proves of how little personal importance a playwriter was esteemed at that day. Halliwell regards this as the "chief period in Shakespeare's literary education, as undoubtedly it was; but it does not follow that it had not been built upon a good foundation, or that it was, during this time, unproductive. If intrinsic proof has any value, Shakespeare's early writings, as well as his later, evince that, however little he may have had in youth of the refinements of culture, he had gone through 'the grind,' and had been put solid on the corner stone of schoolboy Latin, although he never acquired the somewhat unwieldy learning of Ben Jonson and the Universities. But then all the winds of heaven and the angels who make up the ministry of nature were ushers in the school he went to, so that he learned the secrets that make a seer.

Greene, Peele, Nash and Marlowe all died young and disreputably, but they left literary remains that have helped a later inspiration in literature. But contemporary opinion, foreshadowing the verdict of history, is best seen in Ben Jonson's verse. After the death of all these poets, he hesitates not to place Shakespeare first of them all:

> "All tell how far thou didst our Lily out shine,
> Or sporting Kyd, or Marlowe's mighty line."

While he might find in contemporary writers the stimulus of rivalry, the greatest debt Shakespeare owed them was in the instances they afforded his true artistic instinct and practical mind of what to avoid. Doubtless, so far, they were most valuable teachers; but, at all events, they were scarcely more to him than Jane Porter to Scott, or Miss Burney and Fielding to Thackeray and George Eliot—precursors of the dawn.

What are the facts? In 1589, this young man of 21, unable to resist the impulse of genius that called him to a literary career, left his native Stratford for London. The leading actor then in London, Burbage, was a Warwickshire man; and Greene, also a leading member of the *Lord Chamberlain's Players*, to which he probably attached himself, was from Stratford itself. It has been not unreasonably inferred that it was under the patronage of these able men—able in their vocation—that the young adventurer entered on his theatrical career. Fleay says he wrote Venus and Adonis in 1588, though it was not published until 1593; but, in the absence of any proof in the matter, it is not improbable that he brought the poem to London in his pocket, as Sam Johnson long afterwards brought his Irene, with such different (and indifferent) success. It is almost certain that in the next year he was one of a company of players, Lord Strange's, as Fleay concludes, or, as been commonly held, the Lord Chamberlain's, to which he remained attached for a quarter of a century. Three years afterward he was a shareholder in the Globe Company, and later became one of the leading members. We have seen that a play called Hamlet was probably acted in 1586, or 1587, almost certainly in 1588, certainly in 1589. We know that the reputed author proved eventually to be a man of extraordinary genius, of a great facility and fecundity in dramatic production, and that his rise in his profession was phenomenally rapid. While this may have been in some measure due to the charm of his manner and his sterling character, yet his success was primarily and principally professional. He built his reputation and won his position on the solid foundation of merit in the line of his legitimate work—poetry and the drama. Venus and Adonis, which won the admiration of the Court and literary guild from the first, early evinced what a fountain of poesy he possessed; and his plays soon gave him an importance in that branch of the art also. He is said to have been a fair actor in secondary parts, but his usefulness in his company was as the author of plays that won for it wealth, public favor and the first place in the dramatic art. When we regard the metrical and artistic finish of Venus and Adonis, it is incredible that any argument should be based upon the insufficiency of Shakespeare in merely technical skill to accomplish any rhetorical feat at that period.

Despite the objections offered to Shakespeare's ability to write the rough sketch of Hamlet in 1586, at, say, twenty-two years of age, there is nothing in it unprecedented in literature or other walks of life. Pope, who commenced his literary career at sixteen, and published his exquisite Rape of the Lock at twenty-three, might be cited as far more precocious. The wretched, but gifted, Chatterton finished his career by suicide at eighteen. Milton wrote his magnificent Hymn to the Nativity as a college exercise at twenty-one. Burns, Shelley, Byron, Keats, all wrote well at about the same age.

Gerald Griffin had sketched his tragedy of Gisippus when he was fourteen and finished it at eighteen, when the great actor Macready thought it worthy his impersonation; and this was not his only work completed at that age.

And in Shakespeare's own day, his contemporary, Marlowe, showed a like premature genius; while Ben Jonson's first and most successful dramatic work is assigned to his twenty-third year. It really seems strange that any weight should have been attached to this argument. The difficulty at twenty-one, or two, is not in producing a work of the imagination, but in speculative thought, artistic finish and practical dramatic workmanship, in which the earlier Hamlet may well have been deficient. A mere play was not then thought worthy the best efforts of an author, and Hamlet, at first, was probably, in some sort, "a pot boiler." It may be conceded that neither Shakespeare, nor any other man, could have written Hamlet, as we now have it, at such an early age, but we know also that such was not its earliest form, or indeed its form at all, until twelve or fourteen, perhaps sixteen, years later, when life had taught him its lessons.

There is really no *a priori* reason why a man of high order of dramatic genius might not have framed the plot and written an acting play of Hamlet at the age of twenty-two years. But some critics assume that in Shakespeare's case there were personal reasons why he could not then, or ever, have written this, or, indeed, any, of his plays. It is very difficult to argue with gentlemen of this persuasion, as they all feel that they hold a brief—have a cause to maintain. As a characteristic specimen of this sort of estimate of the poet, I give here what Mr. Wm. Henry Smith, in a book entitled, "Bacon and Shakespeare" (Chapter 2nd), calls, "A Brief History of Shakespeare."

"William Shakespeare's is, indeed, a negative history.

Of his life all that we positively know is the period of his death.

We do not know when he was born, nor when, nor where, he was educated.

We do not know when, nor where, he was married, nor when he came to London.

We do not know when, where, or in what order, his plays were written, or performed; nor when he left London.

He died April 23rd, 1616."

That is one way of putting it; it is, indeed, about the sum of the Bacon-Myth argument; and is, in fine, the *reductio ad absurdum* of the whole theory of Shakespeare's nonentity, as based upon negative evidence. And yet if Mr. Smith had been as diligent to find out all that could be known of Shakespeare as he was not to find anything, he might have learned a good many facts, such as they are. Halliwell has shown how much may be known about him through honest investigation. If we do not know the day of his birth, we have the record of his christening, which was then done a few days after, and was considered more essential. We do not know when, nor where, he was educated, but we do know that he entered life armed *cap-a-pie*, able at all points to vanquish, "those twin gaolers of the daring heart, low birth and iron fortune."

The tradition, whatever that is worth, was that

Shakespeare was a lawyer's clerk; and Malone, who first rejected the idea, on fuller examination of the internal evidence, concluded that such was the case. Lord Campbell's citations sustain this view in his monograph, "Legal Acquirements of Shakespeare," though his conclusions are cautiously stated. Lord Campbell adduces a great deal of internal evidence from Shakespeare's plays to prove his familiar knowledge of the law, the fair inference being that he was a "Noverint", so-called, an attorney's clerk, before he left Stratford for London. The Baconians attempt to show that the author of his plays was a wonderful lawyer, and hence was not Shakespeare; but, though his law knowledge seems sound and sure, many attorney's clerks have had more learning and more law.

The evidence summed up by Lord Campbell, Mr. Cartwright and Mr. Heard is, to my mind, as convincing as any such internal evidence can be that Shakespeare was an attorney's clerk, and a good one, in his youth, which was a better education than Dickens had—and yet Lord Macaulay did not write David Copperfield!

Robert Cartwright, in "The Footsteps of Shakespeare", attempts to prove that he studied law, after he came to London, a most improbable theory. But, in doing so, his quotations show Shakespeare's familiarity with law at the time when he wrote Hamlet, and his saturation with legal phrase and thought, that kept coming to the surface. Now, Cartwright assumes that Pericles, Titus Andronicus and the Two Gentlemen of Verona were Shakespeare's first plays, and believes that Hamlet was certainly in existence in 1589, and was most probably written in 1588. The first three plays have few legal indicia, Hamlet a great many; hence he infers that Shakespeare studied law between the production of that first batch and Hamlet. Doubt has been thrown on Shakespeare's authorship of Pericles and Titus Andronicus; and the Two Gentlemen of Verona was probably a collaboration in which he was the junior, though more gifted, partner. If these views are correct, or if his chronology be wrong and Hamlet was written first, Cartwright's argument goes for nothing in favor of the time when he thinks Shakespeare studied law, but for much as to what he knew about it, and as to the close connection between Hamlet and his legal studies. Fresh from his attorney's work at Stratford, when he tried his prentice hand on Hamlet, he then naturally spoke in its terminology. As his experience widened and his vocabulary enlarged, this peculiarity would be less apparent; and, though it might crop out, it would not be obtruded. The display of somewhat cheap classical learning in the Gonzago Play and elsewhere in Hamlet evinces freshness, rather than maturity, in the author, and probably belonged to the first draft of the play. The most valid inference from the legal phraseology that appears so often in Hamlet is that this play was, in some form, one of his earliest productions, if not his very earliest essay in the dramatic art. Is the thought altogether irrational that, because it was his first-born, it retained such a hold on his imagination and affection, and won for itself the birthright, and became the heir of his genius?

Recurring to Mr. Smith's brief and contemptuous "Biography of Shakespeare," we can claim we *do* know when, and where, and whom, he married, and a good deal of such stuff as registers, etc., are made of, about his parents and ancestors and children, and about his mortgages and deeds and his last will. We do not know all about when, where, or in what order, his plays were performed; but we know quite as much of all these and other personal details, as we know concerning a dozen or more of the other leading dramatists of the age. What do we know of any of them? Who then cared for these players and writers? If there was anything evil, or equivocal, in their lives and conduct, be sure that, in the fierce light of religious fanaticism and the burrowing of bookworms, it has a far better chance to escape oblivion than their better deeds.

> "The evil that men do lives after them;
> The good is oft interred with their bones;"

and this is especially true of the Elizabethan dramatists.

In Shakespeare's time, dramatic authors were of small consideration, and, when mentioned, it is the least creditable side of their lives which is turned up to gratify public curiosity; they are to be remembered, it appears, by their follies, their vices and their eccentricities only. Hartley Coleridge, in his Life of Massinger, truly says:

"The lives of our great dramatists, 'of the great

race,' furnish few materials for drama. They are provokingly barren of incident. They present neither complicated plots, nor striking situations, nor well-contrasted characters. In their own age they were overlooked as too familiar—in the next, cast aside as unfashionable."

Dwelling on the immense research that has been brought to bear upon all that concerns those literary giants, he continues: "It is very well that so few reputations have suffered by the scrutiny; for, had the great dramatists been conspicuous for either vice or folly, they would not have shared the fate of the heroes before Agamemnon. They lived in an age of personality. The great eye of the world was not then, any more than now, so intent on things and principles, as not to have a corner for the infirmities of individuals."

"The success or poverty of a dramatist might excite no more sensation than similar vicissitudes in the fortunes of a strolling player, or any other 'unfortunate' living from hand to mouth. Yet less were simple respectability and moderate prosperity calculated for public notice."

The more orderly and uneventful the lives of any of these players, or dramatists, the more likely were they to escape the denunciation of Puritanic play-haters, or the still more fatal admiration of the dissolute reprobates who hung around the purlieus of the theatres. Shakespeare was, therefore, fortunate in coming down to us pictured by the hands of the titanic geniuses who knew him best. As painted by Ben Jonson, the very chief of the literary guild, he was a man of worth, gentle and genial, who sought not fame, but found her nestling at his feet. His good business habits are matters of record, and are best evinced in the fortune he acquired. He retired from a highly successful career in the heydey of his triumphs, at forty six-years of age, to a quiet rural life; and this is the best answer to those who stigmatize him as greedy and dissolute. Most of his contemporaries we know only through their misfortunes. All that is certainly known of Marlowe, Greene, Peele, Beaumont, Fletcher, Massinger, Ford and the rest, even including Ben Jonson, could be printed in a few pages. So that it were strange if Shakespeare's life could not be put into a nutshell. Of the man Shakespeare, we may know but little, if we exclude vague rumor, unverified and conflicting tradition, the gossip of scandal-mongers, and unwarrantable inference. But with his position as an author it is different. We must draw a distinction between the personal and the literary career of writers of that age, or of any age. How much, even in this era of the printing-press, does anybody really know of our great writers? True, there are repositories in biographical dictionaries, magazine articles, etc., from which we can disinter more or less of fact and fiction about them. Blot these out, and write down what you really know about Tennyson, Browning, Anybody. How much is it? What we do really know is what concerns us, their literary value. And, of Shakespeare, we can learn from his contemporaries his place in their esteem as well as if he lived to-day. Ben Jonson sounds no uncertain note in his praise. Harsh, rugged, critical, to others—critical even to Shakespeare—he loved the man, "only this side of idolatry."

Meres tells us, "The sweet witty soul of Ovid lives in mellifluous and honey-tongued Shakespeare." And Weever, still earlier in 1596, also calls him "honey-tongued," and of his works tells us, "Some heaven-born goddess said to be their mother." A Mournful Ditty," on the Queen's death in 1603, calls him "brave Shakespeare;" and the lofty Sir John Davies, in 1607, addresses some verses, "To our English Terence, Mr. Will Shakespeare:"

> "Some say, good Will, which I in sport do sing,
> Had'st thou not played some kingly parts in sport,
> Thou had'st been a companion for a king,
> And been a king among the meaner sort.
> Some others rail; but rail as they think fit,
> Thou hast no railing, but a reigning wit;
> And honestly thou sowest which they do reap,
> So to increase their stock which they do keep."

Which verses may be commended to "some others," who, in this our own day, "rail," as if this man's existence had been a personal grievance to them. In his own day he was reviled, but reviled not again, and that wit, or wisdom, of his, which was acknowledged as regnant, when he was yet but little over two score years of age, by one of the leading writers of the age, reigneth still, and still will reign.

Such, at least as I conceive the facts, were the man and the situation, which may be summed up as follows: the son of a village tradesman—scion of a

family of honest repute, but of decaying fortunes—
growing up amid the influences of rural England,
in one of its manliest and most brilliant epochs,
when it burgeoned and burst into most glorious
blossom, found himself on the threshold of life.
While yet a callow youth, unchecked passions and
the recklessness of the times had burdened him with
a family. Instead of yielding to an almost foregone
fate, he looked up. His mighty gifts, revelations of
genius, far stretching vistas into the invisible realm
of thought and imagination, came to his lowly home
from nature and man and all the voices of the
universe. But, from his whole subsequent career, it
is evident, that with them came a resolve to adjust
all that he was, and all that saw in those upper
realms, to the conditions of his surroundings. He
had the mighty creative faculty, which seems not to
have been denied in some measure to Marlowe and
others, but with it he had also a robust moral nature
and common-sense, and, to speed the keel, an unfail-
ing energy; and it is the union of these qualities that
constitutes genius.

Circumstances, the bent of his inclination, and
that insight which was self-revealing, led him to the
play house. He obeyed the call of destiny. He
became an actor, and thus got his foot into the
stirrup. Not long was it before he was able to
mount Pegasus. In the dreams of his youth, when,
we can believe without shame, a wayward exuber-
ance may have drawn him along with boon companions to play Robin Hood with Sir Thomas Lucy's
deer, as an unverified legend asserts, or even while

poring over the Law French of black letter tomes, he may have caught from nature, or the spiritual universe, or from the very imps of perversity in the crabbed texts themselves, the airs that grew into higher melodies of thought and became immortal dramas. But the Noverint has become a play actor, a hard life, though, at the Elizabethan Court, one with all the inspiration that comes from an atmosphere surcharged with electricity. Plays are needed by his Company ; drunken, reprobate Greene, who sells his plays twice over to rival theatres, cannot be trusted to write them ; Burbage, the leading 'star' of the hour, must have a tragedy. What more likely than that this ambitious tyro should write a play, in imitation of what he had seen in his native village, where we know that dramatic performances had been given while he was still a youth there, or that, following the lead of Lyly, Kyd or Marlowe, he should attempt "a tragedy of blood"—a "Hamlet, Revenge!"

This is such an opportunity as, like the Faery train, is only seen by them to whom the second-sight is given. This young man seizes it ; and, three or four years later, we find him fifth in the list of stockholders of the Company, and already enough known to fame to stir the bile and bitter enmity of disappointed rivals. Henceforth his career was one of uninterrupted success, so that the nickname given in jest became a reality, and he was, in truth, "William the Conqueror."

All of us know something of Shakespeare's method. Plot given, or taken, it may be ; then a play that men will sit through and knit their brows, weep with, perchance, and ponder over, and come again; in a word—a success. And hence we find Hamlet, which should be counted among his earliest plays, as has already been shown, in conception so little dramatic as to its final outcome, if the dramatic consists in action merely, and yet so striking in its isolated situations, and with so self-determined a movement in its essential or intrinsic action. Little care did the bold pioneer in romantic drama take for unities, conventionalities, or the consistency of outward things. Anachronisms, solecisms, historical inaccuracies that would have shocked Baron Verulam, abound in him, but they did not confound him. But then he put men and women, not puppets, upon the stage; and, most of all, he put something of himself, and of the Divine Spirit that moved him, into his characters; and so they live. He was limited by stage requirements needed to render his tragedy a success as an acting play; but, to these, his artistic intuitions and experience on the stage enabled him readily to conform. And beyond this he had the impulse and the constraint of genius to gratify his own creative faculty and power of large discourse, "looking before and after." This was a law of his being, as Maker, Master, Wizard, Sovereign Elect of the Drama, and, as it would seem, of all literature.

No greater damage could then be done a troop of players than to print their plays, and thus rob them of their monopoly of acting them. They were addressed to the senses, the eye and ear, and not to that more subtle communion with the intelligence through the printed page. It was the habit of these companies to take any old, or popular, story, and give such a version of it as suited the conditions of the case, the times, the audience, the abilities of the actors, and, to a small extent, the spectacular effect. What this legend of Hamlet was, and who was the prototype of the Prince of Denmark, I shall discuss later on. But at first it was only a cartoon that he sketched. It seems certain that anybody's suggestion, interpolation, or addition, if clearly an improvement to a play, would be freely accepted. Literary jealousies and sensibilities had small place in compositions chiefly anonymous, among a co-operative company, where gain and joint dramatic success were the prime objects. This was the advantage that the young and obscure, but gifted, man would have. His utility would be readily recognized, and he would speedily become indispensable.

Shakespeare, like other dramatists of his day, took his plots in the main as he found them. He was not solicitous, or too careful, as to the material on which he was to imprint the seal of his genius. Marble or sandstone, Corinthian brass or cherry stones, were indifferent to him. The crude, refractory stuff would become precious with the signature, 'W. Shakespeare.' This is not to say that Shakespeare thought of the matter thus, or did himself justice therein, but it is to state a fact. He took his plots from anywhere, recast them to suit the exigencies of the play-house, and then, with the transmuting force of his genius, conformed them to the eternal verities.

Let us suppose, then, that Shakespeare made a sketch, as we would now term it, of this tragedy; and that in 1586 or 1587 his company put it, such as it was, upon the stage. Every representation of it might bring with it some alteration which his own dramatic intuitions, or the expertness of actors, would suggest, so that, at last, the play would crystallize into the shape in which we have it in the First Quarto, and in which it probably held the stage, until about 1596, when it seems to have fallen for a time into obscurity. In 1586, Hamlet was to Shakespeare a youth of twenty; only two years his junior, his dear younger brother and confidant—perhaps in some degree, his own image or double;—in 1596, Hamlet had become a man of thirty, who had chewed the bitter-sweet cud of life, and who had seen, too, its illusions shattered. Hamlet developed by just so much as Shakespeare did.

It is probable that Shakespeare thus in 1596 again took up this fruitage of his springtime, and, under social, political and personal conditions entirely different from those of its original conception, elaborated it to the comprehensive scope of the Second Quarto, or Last Hamlet. This was apparently at a crisis in his life.

Hamlet seems, from the profound melancholy which pervades its soliloquies, which, indeed, underlies it, to have been written in a season of defeat to its author. This may have been in part some reverse of fortune, or threat of disaster, of the details of which we are not aware. But as the dissatisfaction is spiritual, rather than material, it is more probable that this gloom resulted from the awakening of a high and noble spirit to a consciousness of its own defects, limitations, and moral reverses, and from an unavailing struggle for an outlet from the valley of the shadow of death.

The pessimism in this play has been accounted for by the death of his only son in 1596, and the loss of other near and dear relations about that time. Political and financial events may have contributed to it. Self-reproach for a life which had not been regulated by an absolute standard of right, perhaps, more than both of these, bred those doubtings, questionings, and moral defiances to a universe with the law and perfection of which he was not in accord.

Mr. W. W. Story thus gracefully puts forward a suggestion that has occurred to others as well as himself.

"He is as perfectly impersonal as a mirror held up to nature.

> 'He nor commends nor grieves,
> Pleads for itself the fact,
> As unrelenting Nature leaves
> Her every act.'

Yet here and there one seems to catch a personality, and this last citation brings one to my mind. There is always a certain insistence on the delight of men living, and a certain horror of death, which seems to me to show that to him life was a great joy, and death to his active nature had a peculiar repulsion. One sees this constantly in Hamlet, which is, perhaps, the least impersonal of all the characters he ever drew, and represents a mood which comes to all imaginative natures at a certain period of life, and through which he was passing when he wrote this play. The sphinx riddle of humanity, and of life and death, was then troubling his reason and his consciousness, and so weighing upon him that it gives a color to all the meditations of Hamlet that is doubtless completely true to Hamlet dramatically, but that has a certain somewhat beyond the dramatical truth and of a personal character. I cannot exactly explain why this is, but I cannot help feeling it." (Story's Conversations in a Studio, vol. I. page 113).

Though Shakespeare's only son Hamnet was the namesake, as well as the godson, of his early friend, Hamnet Sadler, and Hamlet was the name used in the old story on which the play was based, still the coincidence has some significance, especially if we admit that Shakespeare made his first draft of the tragedy soon after the birth of his son. It seems that about that time this legend of Hamlet must somehow have fastened itself upon his imagination, and engaged his prentice hand. But the coincidence of Hamnet's death in 1596 with Shakespeare's revival of interest in his early production at that time is more remarkable. For some reason, as we may judge from internal evidences in his works, this was a critical period, and, to some extent, a turning point, in his career. He took up Hamlet again with no boyish hand, but with the grasp and power that have made it a world poem.

None can tell how much this man had built upon the future of his only son. It is the quality of ambitious, imaginative, altruistic, natures to go out of themselves in their dreams of advancement. Shakespeare felt that his profession and the hard conditions of his fate had shut him out from the full rewards of his genius in his own generation. All the traditions and prejudices of his country and time pointed to the establishment of his family—the founding of a house—as the most legitimate and honorable aim of a man in his, or any, position. It is easy to recall Sir Walter Scott's similar fruitless dream of Abbotsford and a county family. This was the meaning of Shakespeare's thrift, his wish for wealth, his purchases of land, his claim to a coat of arms, his aspiration to be a country gentleman. But his dear boy died, and all was shattered. His dream was dissolved. He was alone, 'a barren sceptre in his gripe', with no son to stand in the gate and uphold his name. Men speak of the bitterness of death; but the bitterness of life!—we will not speak of it.

It is likely also that the friends at Court, on whom he counted, he found cold, or, in the crooked cabals of the time, thwarted in his and their designs. But, again, it is only too probable, from the internal evidences of the sonnets and from traditions that have come down to us, and from the very nature of things, that he had not held himself entirely aloof from the temptations of life, and, having tasted the cup of sin, that he had to drink its bitter dregs in repentance. Thus we may readily conceive how the vision of this full orbed single soul could, with such large discourse, behold the soul of man, and mirror it, and manifest it to us in this self-revelation.

An entry in the Stationer's Register in 1602, speaks of a proposed copy of Hamlet, "as it was *lately* acted." The Clarendon Editors infer from this that

Hamlet then enjoyed only a recent popularity ; but to me it seems that this implies that improvements, or changes, had then recently been introduced into its earlier versions. All along he had been putting more of his dramatic art, his stage experience, and his knowledge of life, into it, as it grew to the clear and definite proportions of the first Quarto. But now into this Revision in the Second Quarto, the last Hamlet, he put himself. He thoroughly saturated it with his own personality, and, by the interpenetration of his own entity with the wavering shape of the Danish Prince, gave his great tragedy its present poetic and magnificent form. The volcanic flashes of his genius reveal profoundest depths, intellectual and moral, of their source—the perturbed spirit of the author. How the gems of Shakespeare's rationality came to be imbedded in that strange, crude, barbarous, old legend, may then be best accounted for, according to our conviction, by the *evolution* of this tragedy of Hamlet. Evolution ! Yes, it is just in this fact that Hamlet was an evolution, Shakespeare's evolution and not another's, that most of the difficulties of the play, its inconsistencies and contradictions of action, character and incident, may be explained, and in some degree removed. To its genesis and growth, it owes its perennial interest. "Born, not made :" trite, but powerful expression of the immeasurable difference between dead matter and living force ! Springing up from some germ dropped into the fecund imagination of the poet, it grows with his growth, and draws its sap and fibre from the storm and sunshine of his soul ; and, at last, it becomes a mighty monarch of the forest, like the cedar that guards the slopes of Libanus, or the gigantic redwood that towers in our own Yosemite, or some Druidical oak of its native soil. It has stood in our literature now for more than three centuries, and the magic circle of its shadows still fall upon the heart with the same, or a deeper, sense of mystery and spiritual meaning than when it first came into being. So that the perfect Hamlet—at first the picture of a particular man, as I conceive, and then the mirror of all mankind—fully justifies the claim made for it in my former lecture to pre-eminence as the greatest creation of the greatest poet the world has ever seen.

THE PLOT OF HAMLET.

"This play is the image of a murther done in——?
Hamlet, III. 2.

Though this be madness, yet there is method in it."
Hamlet, II, 2.

In my lecture on "The Significance of Hamlet," I believe I evinced no low estimate of the tremendous mystery and meaning of this mighty drama of the Human Will. If I have succeeded in apprehending these aright, it is by following in the footsteps of powerful and profound intellects of an older generation, availing myself of their suggestions, and attempting to arrive at somewhat more exact and definite results. If others arrive at a different result, it would seem childish to quarrel with them for opinions on a subject so impersonal, and, I might say, so intangible. Still, as the *odium theologicum* appears to seize on so many Shakespearian commentators, one would feel a nervous dread of advancing any criticism, if sensitive to personal animadversion. Hence, I ought to say in this connection that, while rejecting the Baconian Paradox, it is still with very great respect for the industry, ingenuity, acumen and logic of many advocates and adherents of that school. I am forced to believe the whole theory erroneous, groundless, but I attribute the error of its disciples, not to a lack of reasoning power, but to this or that mistake in the premises. Statements are accepted as facts which rest upon little evidence, and, from these, large inferences are made ; but the argumentation is vigorous enough when once set going. Its advocates reason as if they held a brief in the case.

This preamble m be the more necessary as I am myself in this lecture about to venture upon a theory which has not met acceptance at the hands of the critics, even when it has attracted their attention, and which has been issed by a recent able writer, the author of "The stery of Hamlet," with supercilious contempt. Now, while I am quite willing to concede that any new, or disputed, point in Shakespearian criticism should be advanced with becoming diffidence, nevertheless, I must frankly submit what I conceive to be the most probable explanation of the origin of the play of Hamlet. If I am in error in this view, I shall still hope to show that there is something in it that deserves consideration at least.

The significance of the play of Hamlet involves one of the great problems of human existence. Shakespeare has put this problem into the mechanism and action of the drama, and it enlists our interest and holds our intellects attent, as when the sculptor makes the marble speak to the inner sense of the beholder, or the architect builds a poem and a creed into the bricks and mortar of some grand cathedral. But it does not necessarily follow that the origin of the play was upon a plan in which the details from the first filled out the broad lines of the large theme. Such is not, as a rule, the genesis of the greatest creations of literary genius. The grandest results are not those which spring from the most ambitious designs. Not the subject, but the treatment, lends dignity. The material employed is often but the common clay of our humanity, intended for mere homely uses; it is the inspiration of the Divine Reason that enables the poet to render it sublime. His large discourse, his lofty imagination, and his soulful energy seize upon a story—a crude legend perhaps, or a trivial plot—and represent the persons who share in it, and it grows to greatness under his hand, as its phases reveal the interaction of emotion, intellection and will. It becomes the unconscious display of the poet's own spirit in his work, and hence an ideal in art.

What I am leading up to is that it was not necessary for Shakespeare to analyze and consciously formulate his whole theory of Being—to perceive clearly the image of the human mystery in Hamlet—to see reflected there in its magic mirror the full-size likeness of himself—when he made the first draft of his stage play. It was born, it grew, it became the splendid flower of his genius. But, at first, it was a play meant for the stage, though probably intended for other purposes, as well as for mere amusement. Its immediate purpose may have been to instruct a particular audience; but it contained enough of wisdom for its voices to reach out to all mankind. "Their line has gone out through all the earth, and their words to the end of the world."

All the comment and criticism on the character of Hamlet has not gone much deeper than Goethe's thought, though a fuller unfolding of it may give us a better comprehension of him. And here the question may be started, how did Shakespeare come to conceive, to create, such a *character?* And, again, how did *Shakespeare* come to conceive such a character? Pregnant questions, but not unanswerable! For answer, we must look to the times, the environment, the antecedents. Few will deny the influence of prevalent thought—of the Time-Spirit—and of the moulding activity of the environment upon literary production. To these, Shakespeare was amenable. They are seen in his quips, in his grossness, in his euphuism, in the turn and trick of his phrase, in the quick, lambent fire of his thought, in the audacity and largeness of his imagination. The age just gone by had been an era of revolt and overthrow. Protestantism had hurled down the Church of Rome in England, and new forms, institutions, doctrines and modes of thought had rushed in to supplant the old. The England of Elizabeth was a new world, a rebuilding of society. Strange things were in the air. Drake was sweeping the Spanish Main, and Raleigh planting the English race on a virgin continent. Bacon was building a new philosophy; and Puritanism and Parliamentary government, in the search for truth and justice, were hardening their sinews for later strife and triumph. All was astir, in confusion. Had chaos come again? Not so, for a surety. But all things were in question—facts, creeds, philosophies; and yet reason still remained as Chief Inquisitor. What men sought was to build not upon shams and delusions, but upon the Truth. But, "What is Truth?" O, question of the ages, first asked with lisping tongue by primeval man; most memorably demanded of Him, who standing before a Roman tribunal, was Himself the answer! Yes, this was, and is, the question. Bishop Butler says: "I mean to make truth the business of my life;" and Nathaniel W. Taylor tells us, "Let us be true; this is the highest maxim of art and of life, the secret of eloquence and virtue, and of all moral authority." And these are but faint modern echoes of Ridley and Latimer, who lighted two candles in England that have not since gone out; as, indeed, these again were but reverberations of Epictetus and St. Paul. The Norman mind, intensely egotistic and independent, was also subtle, intellectual and religious. It had shaped the thought of England to chronic protest and revolt against all alien domination, temporal and spiritual. In that great revolt, the Protestant Reformation, every element in England concurred. Its power was as a *national* contest. Patriotism, love of liberty, the passion for fame and the energy of individual enterprise fenced the throne of Elizabeth with the swords of gentle and simple alike. So that, as a rule, the great mass of those even who adhered to the old religion were Englishmen first and pre-eminently; and, though there were fanatics of another kidney, the Catholic lords and yeomen rose to resist the Armada. So the Puritan Stubbs, whose hand had been stricken off for freedom of speech, waved the bloody stump, as he shouted, "God save Queen Elizabeth!"; and his comrade who suffered with him sturdily cried out, "There lies an honest English hand!" The freedom of the individual spirit to seek, and to find, the way, the truth, and the life, was implicit in the new gospel, in whatever forms it may have been couched. England was never more enthusiastically English than then.

Shakespeare, an observer, a thinker, a maker, but always too, an Englishman, and young and ardent, was in the very maelstrom of English thought and feeling. To him, as to every high soul, the question comes : "Man : what, why, whence, whither?" "I, too," says Arcturus, "Will cast my ray into the black abyss, and enlighten the darkness." But not a star in all the firmament, save the Day-Spring from on high, can do more than make this darkness visible. When all are reaching out blindly toward the Infinite, shall the master-thinker—the Seer—hold back his hand? Shall he not vaticinate? What is truth? What is man? Is there a metaphysical order in the universe? Is Fate all? Is free-will naught? Do the books tell it? Have the priests solved it? Such is the virgin skepticism that with reverent hand, in Shakespeare, lifts the curtain of the unknown. Into Hamlet's sad musings, Shakespeare projected his own soul and the spirit of his times, but he has also evinced prophetic vision, and heralded the dominant idea of the coming centuries. He it was, no less than the philosophers, preachers and martyrs, who with sweetest accent ushered in the phantom doubt, that has since so stirred and guided modern thought. His wand evoked Goethe, it trained Darwin and Spencer, and disciplined Kingsley and Dean Stanley. And, O inconceivable thought! that this arch-magician should be but a playright! In the eternal fitness of things, how could he be less than an Inductive Philosopher, an Apothegmatic Essayist, and a Lord Chancellor and Viscount St. Albans?

Is it possible for us to discover now why this play was written, for what purpose, to what end? To amuse! Surely—but no more? To instruct! Indubitably—but whom, wherefore? The World! Yes. the world, large and small; that little world, the Court of his puissant and high-stomached princess, the Virgin Queen, and those other millions who have since soliloquized with Hamlet and wept with the fair Ophelia. But was there no great personage to whom the lesson of Hamlet might carry a present lesson of special significance, to whom it might be a matter of pith and moment; and was there no coterie to whose policy its teachings might render acceptable service? Perhaps it may be difficult to prove this in manner and form, to demonstrate it beyond controversy; but, in the prevalent nebulosity about Shakespeare's plays, and the natural interest every aspect of them excites, some suggestions on these points may not be unacceptable, which the diligent antiquarian may, if he please, afterwards work out to fruitful results.

In the study of Shakespeare's plays, not only the method of his art engages us, but this *wherefore!* Why Hamlet, and not something else? Why did Shakespeare write this particular play in this particular way, at the particular point of time when it was first acted? To some minds accident is a sufficient cause, and we do, indeed, find insignificant things often the proximate causes of great events. But most causes are adequate; and the more adequate, the more explicable are they. In considering the production of a play and its *raison d'être*, it is not amiss to recollect not only the literary skill and method of the author, but what manner of man he was. I have already tried in few words to depict the Elizabethan epoch as an era of awakening, the leafy June of English thought. I have described Shakespeare, too, as a high-souled poet and consummate artist, a seer to whom all the windows of the soul were open, from the outlooks of which a thousand vistas of the world of man declared themselves to his vision. Such is the poet, as he stands like Moses upon Horeb, and as we see him in the fullness of his intellectual stature. But when his pontifical robes are cast aside, and he descends into the arena of actual life, we find that Shakespeare was a man of affairs too; nay, even a man about town; he was a writer with a patron, a writer for a patron; he was also an active member of a stage company, playing second best parts, but adapting, even composing, immortal dramas. But, most of all, he was an Englishman, and, as such, both a patriot and a politician. His patriotism breathes through the mighty music of his dramas, even as the undertone comes to us, in the awful rush and roar of waters at Niagara. He puts into the mouth of Falconbridge, one of his favorites and a most typical Englishman the words:

> "This England never did, and never shall,
> Lie at the proud foot of a conqueror,
> But when it first did help to wound itself."
> *King John*, V. 7.

Public affairs were neither unknown, nor uncared for by him. He had a right to feel an interest in them. Was not his father, the wool-stapler, "of the corporation of the borough?" By birth he belonged to that sturdy middle-class, which, by patient, persistent resolution, has wrung its liberties from Crown and nobles, and with them the control of England. But, though, as a strolling player, he had swung away from his local moorings and parish politics, he had drifted into that vast pool, the Court and its purlieus, in which all the great movements of the realm were matters of keenest personal interest. In that brilliant circle of versatile Bohemians, "the Queen's poor players," to which he belonged, all questions of political moment, as well as the artistic side of life, were discussed with vivid curiosity. They were, as a rule, the dependents, or partisans, of some powerful and munificent patron, and were warmed or chilled as the sunshine of royalty fell upon, or was withdrawn from, their Maecenas. In modern political phrase, they were his "henchmen;" and their duty was not only to amuse the leisure, but oftentimes to serve the purposes or advance the fortunes, of their chief. This is illustrated in this very tragedy of Hamlet, when the Player King and his company perform a part not found in the rôles of dramatic companies— "to catch the conscience of the King." To his company of players, a politic patron might very well commit the delicate task of conveying an unwelcome truth in pleasing form, or of suggesting lines of action that might not be declared, or of hinting in allegory what he might wish attempted in action.

In 1586, the point of time at which we will assume that the first draft of the play of Hamlet was conceived, the political horizon was lowering, and a death struggle seemed imminent between the party of reaction and the English Court. The former centred its hopes on the captive Queen of Scots; while England, apart from the papistical faction, looked to Elizabeth as the pole-star in the political firmament. War with Rome existed in England, though undeclared and waged with poison and poignard only; but none the less war, because tacit and with conspiracy as the strategy of closet and council chamber. High and mighty ones advised the assassination of Elizabeth, and she herself tried to instigate the jailers of the Queen of Scots to murder her privately after her condemnation.

Plot followed plot, all to end abortively under the lynx-eyed vigilance of Burleigh and Walsingham. The Duke of Norfolk, two Earls of Northumberland, William Parry, and others, perished because of their attempts; but, in 1586, the formidable conspiracy, known as "Babington's", brought matters to a head. Mary Stuart was regarded as the centre of the machinations aimed at the life and throne of Elizabeth, whose masculine spirit and genius for finesse did not shrink from the death-grapple. Without pronouncing here on the right or wrong of this intricate question, from the point of view of the English Council and Court and of the patriot faction, and, possibly, of Elizabeth herself, the death of Queen Mary had become necessary to secure her safety and the peace and glory of England. I do not say that this view was correct, but it was that of the worldly-wise councilors of Elizabeth, and, so far as success justifies policy, it has such further sanction. The national party, as well as enthusiastic Protestants, believed in and supported this course.

You must permit me here to assume, without argument, as correct, the view of Froude, based, in part, upon the representations of Chasteauneuf, the French Ambassador to the King of France: "The Council and people generally," he said, "were earnest that she should be executed, but he did not think Elizabeth herself would consent to extremities if she could help it." Secretary Davison confirmed the opinion of the French Ambassador.

It is very difficult to decide positively by what name the Company went to which Shakespeare first attached himself, nor is to it our present purpose; whether Lord Leicester's, Lord Strange's, the Queen's, or the Lord Chamberlain's, matters very little. Leicester and Lord Hunsdon, the Lord Chamberlain, were almost equally involved in the proceedings against Mary, and in the Council voted for her condemnation and execution. And, though the Stanleys were Catholic, Lord Strange's father, Lord Derby, was a violent Loyalist, and rallied to Elizabeth when the Spanish Armada was threatening. The patrons of Shakespeare and his fellow-players were, from whatever motives, hostile to the Queen of Scots, and we find Shakespeare attached through life to, what might be called, in such a network of intrigue as the Court of Elizabeth presented, the National Party, or to that branch of it at least that Leicester and Essex headed. Southampton, his patron, was Essex's nearest friend. When Mary fell however, Burghley, Walsingham, Leicester, the noble Sussex, Hunsdon, and many more, felt that a hard necessity required her death. Let us suppose this inchoate policy taking shape. Suppose the execution of Queen Mary settled upon, or discussed even, as the true cutting of a tangled political knot, and we may safely assume that these far-sighted and ambidextrous statesmen would neglect no means to justify so audacious a stroke, or at very least to try the temper of that doubtful middle opinion that counts for so much. This was to be reconciled. After the execution these arguments became the more necessary in view of the attitude of Elizabeth, who repudiated all responsibility for it, and when her chief councilors were in peril of life and property from her.

But there was another factor that could not be disregarded, namely, King James of Scotland. James was the son of the woman whose death upon the scaffold was foredoomed. It is hard to conceive any line of argument, or set of circumstances, that would wring from this champion of the divine right of kings a compromise with regicide, or from a son even a tacit assent to his mother's ignominious execution. But Elizabeth knew her man. Great is Ego always; but, in that cold heart and clear, tortuous brain, Self reigned supreme. First of all, he was a Stuart, which always meant a multitude of meannesses, and a mass of littlenesses. He was King of Scotland too, and heir presumptive to the throne of England by grace of the Great Queen, under whose wing he dodged and fluttered as a sub-King or Kinglet,—a stripling prince of twenty—the sole royal chick in her brood of aspirants. By her support he maintained his authority over a turbulent nobility; and his mother's imprisonment, or death, was the only sure guaranty of his privilege to reign at all. His title was defeasible quite, if Queen Mary got the upper hand. Such an event would upset his throne, and even put in peril his sacred person, so precious to himself; for questions would be started that the sword alone could settle. It is well known that Mary's resentment at his alliance with Elizabeth induced her to assent to a plan for his capture and deposition. His only real safety lay in the protection of England. Nevertheless, a King is a piece on the national chessboard not to be despised;—nay, even a Kinglet, if he be a son and a man, must be taken into account. The crooked Cecilian policy, looking to James as its future monarch, owed to him this deference, that a fair plea be made for its harsh deed, as a sop to the royal conscience, if no more. To this end, it is probable, no argument was omitted, nor any means neglected. True, Elizabeth hated James, as the son of her rival and her own rightful heir, but she was too wise to ignore him. To James and to the world, then, must be justified the hard necessity, the cruel compulsion, of the bloody deed.

The Master of Gray, James' go-between with the English Government, which had bought him, writing to Archibald Douglas, September 18, 1586, says, of the king: "His opinion is it cannot stand with his honor that he be a consenter to take his mother's life, but he is content how strictly she be kept, and all her old knavish servants hanged, chiefly they that be in hands. For this you must deal warily to eschew inconvenients, seeing necessity of all honest men's affairs requires *she was taken away.*" (Froude, History of England, XII. 292).

Every plea, direct and indirect, would be put forth. We know that both money and promises were used, and Sir Robert Carey, son of Shakespeare's patron, the Lord Chamberlain Hunsdon, was sent on a special mission to placate the wounded honor of king James. Among other agencies, the stage might well be employed for the teaching of important political object lessons. A play that should stir the minds and hearts of the Court, then the center of intellectual and political activity, against the unhappy captive queen, was an engine too powerful to be overlooked. Nor was James, with his fondness for pageantry and the theatre, apt to disregard such teaching. The vivid presentation of a case, odious indeed, yet closely analogous to Mary's own, might make that queen appear to him as the victim of a just retribution. It has already been pointed out that in this very tragedy of Hamlet a play is interpolated, as in Shakespeare's conception a proper political device. Such a device was not foreign to his ideas, or to the resources of diplomacy. The powerful tragedy of Edward II, by Christopher Marlowe, was also produced about this time; Warton thinks it was written in 1590. It may have been earlier; but, whether written before or after the execution of Mary, Queen of Scots, it was a similar case of the killing of a king with the connivance of his guilty queen, another blast to blow into flame the popular indignation against such naughty deeds, and to palliate, excuse, or justify, such a doubtful political act as the execution of the sovereign of a sister country.

We find this use of the play, as well as of other forms of literature, for political purposes, quite frequent in English history. Plumptre cites Rowe's Tamerlane in 1702, Addison's Cato in 1713, Mallet's Elvira in 1763, and the Fall of Mortimer in the same year, as notable instances of this appliance; and the reader can recall many instances, in our own day, of the same kind; for instance, the Octoroon and Uncle Tom's Cabin.

England was on fire with loyal zeal and Anti-Papist rage; and it is not unlikely that a young, impulsive and ardent soul, the playwright Shakespeare, should share in the general patriotic delirium, in which all classes were involved. On Mary's trial (if such it can be called), the charges against her were that she had "conspired the destruction of Queen Elizabeth and of England and the subversion of religion."

Parliament in an address to the Queen, November 5th, 1586, urged that the sentence upon the Queen of Scots be immediately carried into execution, "because, upon advised and grave consultation, we cannot find that there is any possible means to provide for your Majesty's safety, but by the just and speedy death of said Queen."

"When the judgment of the Commissioners was proclaimed in London by sound of trumpet, the bells tolled many peals for twenty-four hours, bonfires blazed in the streets, and the citizens appeared intoxicated with joy, as if a great victory had been obtained over a foreign enemy. These rejoicings were redoubled on the news of her execution." (Campbell's Lord Chancellors, v. 2, p. 123).

In extracts from the "Register of the Stationers" (Vol. 2, p. 145), we find, as early as May 30, 1581, licensed to Garrath James, a ballad, declaring the Treason conspired against the King of Scots.

In the entries of 1587, we find a number of ballads and pamphlets justifying the execution of Mary, Queen of Scots; among others, "An excellent ditty made as a general rejoicing for the cutting off the Scottish Queen", licensed nineteen days after her death.

On the 8th of August, 1587, was licensed, "A ditty of Lord Darnley, sometime King of Scots."

Mary was executed February 1, 1587. In the eyes of Shakespeare and of the English people, the plots against Elizabeth in the name of the deposed Queen were acts of treason and rebellion. To them the captive was but a conspirator, while Elizabeth was queen, *the* queen, and poor Mary's taking off seemed but the just penalty of attempted regicide. This and the murder of Darnley are the crimes to which the author points as demanding retribution. It is to this view and these feelings, that we must attribute such passages as the following:

"There's such a divinity, etc." (Act iv, S. 5, L. 118).

"The single and peculiar life is bound, etc." (Act iii, S. 3, L. 10.)

The latter of these quotations, however, is not in

the First Quarto, and may very well have been added much later to please the absolutist tendencies of either James or Elizabeth.

When Mary's head had fallen on the block, whatever may have been Elizabeth's real sentiments, we know that she utterly repudiated the act, disgraced her secretary Davison, sent Burleigh to the Tower, and ominously hinted that but for their services she would have had the heads of Burleigh, Walsingham and Leicester. Now was the time then for them and their friends to bestir themselves, and, if Hamlet was not produced before that time, there was a pressing exigency in which it might well do good service. We cannot say positively that it was at this moment that it first appeared, but it would seem a time when a reason for it is most evident.

Let us assume now that the policy of Mary's execution had been determined upon or had even been carried out, and that the Lord Chamberlain, or the Earl of Leicester, or Lord Hundson, should give a hint that a play on such a theme, with plot pointed out or left to the invention of the playwright as we may decide, would be most graciously received, and, indeed, munificently rewarded. Whoever else may have been called to stir in this matter, we may rest assured that the hand of one William Shakespeare was pre-eminent therein. The era of dramatic incubation had dawned. Ten years later, about 1596, new plays, tragedies, comedies, pastorals, masques, revels, what not, were hatched like spring chickens —forty in less than two years in the theatres in which this Shakespeare, then at the head of his profession, was actor, manager, or playwright. But even now he was recognized as a power. He may have been a pot-hunter in literature, writing for bread or gold, but then and always he was a Titan. Without doubt he was the lawyer's clerk, yclept by the jealous Nash, "a Noverint," who had a hand in the tragedy, the burthen whereof was "Hamlet! Revenge!" If anything could make us doubt this fact, it would be, as has been said, the dissent of such critics as Richard Grant White and the Clarendon editors; but, though it may put us in a quandary to disagree with them, the weight of evidence seems for Shakespeare's authorship. Indeed, assuming the First Quarto to represent this version, as in substance it most probably does, though enlarged, improved and developed, we may say we *know* Shakespeare wrote it; just as we say Michael Angelo did this and Raphael this, because no other could; just as we say, this is the work of the lightning, this of the whirlwind, and this of the ocean, because heaven employs no less agencies for such effects. So, if we find the first Hamlet unequal to Shakespeare's best handiwork, yet we know it to be his, because it is better than the best of other men. But this first draft must be regarded as the sapling which grew into a giant oak, with arms ever sturdier and unfolding a finer foliage.

Let us suppose our author to have received his commission. If it please any idolater better, let him believe the spring of it to have been in Shakespeare's own national, patriotic and Protestant feeling. But we must not forget that, however honest a man he may have been, he was by profession a courtier's courtier, the minister in a minor court. It may be remembered that the "Midsummer Night's Dream" contains an allusion to a mermaid, supposed to be aimed at Mary Stuart, coupled with a compliment to Elizabeth, as "a fair vestal,"—though this was probably written in 1592. The poet, however, has received his inspiration from heaven or the Council. A play is wanted that will fit the case ; broad in its bearings, stirring in its incidents, human enough in its relations to call a halt in thought, and yet subtle to touch this particular grievance of royal assassination to the quick with fatal suggestion. What shall the plot be? First of all, the murder of a king, and the marriage of his widow with the murderer—and then there must needs be a young prince, who in the mazes of doubt is called to revenge.

If Shakespeare desired a pattern for Hamlet, or for Darnley's death, he might have found it, indeed may have heard of it, in the curious spectacle enacted before the Lords at Stirling, within a fortnight after Mary's marriage to Bothwell.

Among the letters of Sir Wm. Drury to Cecil is one quoted by Miss Strickland (Queens of Scotland, Vol. 5, 265), in which he says, May 26, 1567 : "There hath been an interlude of boys played at Stirling, which hath much offended the Earl of Bothwell, for the same was the manner of the king's death, and the arraignment of the Earl, who in the play he that did represent him was hanged, meaning but in sport." The boy player was, as it appears, hanged too long, and came near dying.

There is a rude old legend in Saxo Grammaticus,

known to learned clerks, which Belleforest, after a fashion, put into French in his "*Histoires Tragiques*, about 1570; which again was translated into English, as the "Hystorie of Hamblet." This was court literature, and the story seems made to hand to suit the case of James and his mother. But, if it miscarry, after all what is it but a fable, done over for the stage, and no scandal meant? Under feigned names, poor, base, vicious, handsome Darnley, a royal simulacrum, shall come back in this day dream to a more real life, as "my father's ghost," and bloody Bothwell, that "adulterate beast," shall live again as the felon king. And the queen?—the queen! There is, alas, but one queen whose unhappy fate has been to marry with her husband's murderer, and she is now in the toils, and Nemesis glides on the stage. Hamlet? In this Prince of Denmark, "that unmatched form and feature of blown youth," whom shall all men see but that fair bud of royal promise, the modern Solomon, the young King James, who, with his quiddities and bookish ways, may even himself, perchance, perceive his own princely likeness in this looking glass. Some commentators have even believed that they have found the pattern of Polonius in Lord Burleigh, Sir Nicholas Throckmorton, or other of Elizabeth's Council, and, it may be also, of Rosencrantz and Guildenstern and Osric in the minions and butterflies of the Court. *Sans doute*, had we the chance to parley with some shrewd maid of honor of that day, we would know it all. We have been told, I believe, that Essex, or Sir Philip Sidney, sat for the portrait of Hamlet. But we have not so far to go;

for Shakespeare's picture of the heir of Denmark is more than a likeness, it is the very counterpart, of the heir of England. In King James we may find the prototype of Hamlet.

I cannot hope to establish this claim unchallenged ; but, having exhibited what I conceive to be a sufficient political motive for the production of this play, before entering on a consideration of the plot I beg leave to note the following circumstances. Some twenty years ago I observed the striking points of likeness in the murder of Darnley to the plot of Hamlet, and the resemblance of James and Hamlet in character, and supposed that the discovery was original with me. I subsequently found, however, that nearly a century ago the Rev. Mr. Plumptre had pointed out some of the more obvious of these parallelisms. Though I have the pamphlet, Furness' succinct statement of the points in Plumptre's pamphlet gives its substance with sufficient clearness ; and this I quote, in order to accord due credit to the first finder, especially as he set great store by his discovery. I subjoin Carl Silberschlag's paradoxical additions to it.* Furness says :

"In 1796, James Plumptre, M.A., published some observations on Hamlet, etc., being an attempt to prove that (Shakespeare) designed (this tragedy) as an indirect censure on Mary, Queen of Scots. In this volume the author assumes that since Shakespeare in 1592 did not hesitate, in the Midsummer Night's Dream, to compliment Elizabeth at the expense of Mary, he would have no scruples in still

* Furness' Variorum Hamlet, Vol. 11, p. 236.

further flattering his royal mistress in 1596 (the date when Hamlet was written), by adding his drop to the flood of calumny poured out over her rival. This hypothesis obliges him to maintain that the Queen in Hamlet was an accessory to her husband's death."

"Plumptre adduces the following passages and allusions to show that Shakespeare had Mary, Queen of Scots, directly in mind when he wrote them ; 'In second husband let me be accursed ! None wed the second but who killed the first,' (III. ii, 169 ;) and 'The instances that second marriage move are base respects of thrift, but none of love.'—(Ib. 172), 'which, says the author, 'appear to be so strongly marked as almost of themselves to establish the hypothesis.' Next, Gertrude's haste to marry the murderer of her husband. Lord Darnley was murdered on the 10th February, 1567, and Mary was married to Bothwell on the 14th of May following, a space of time but just exceeding three months. Lord Darnley was the handsomest young man in the kingdom, but of a weak mind ; it is remarkable in Hamlet no compliment is paid to the murdered king's intellectual qualities. Bothwell was twenty years older than Mary, and is represented as an ugly man by the historians. He was also noted for his debauchery and drinking, two circumstances which Shakespeare seems never to lose sight of in his character of Claudius. Ophelia's allusion to the 'beauteous majesty of Denmark,' IV. v., Plumptre says is inapplicable to Gertrude, because 'she was past the prime of life, not to say old,' whereas it applies most justly to Mary, who was only forty-five when she was beheaded, and very beautiful. In the beginning of Hamlet the hero is represented as very young, but in the graveyard we are told that he was thirty years old. 'James was just thirty at the writing of this play.' Whereupon Plumptre remarks: 'Shakespeare seems to have been so blinded by the circumstances he wished to introduce that he has fallen into many improbabilities between his two plans.' Shakespeare mentions the King as having been taken off, "in the blossom of his sin," 'which,' says Plumptre, 'is incompatible with the ideas we have of the King's *age* in the play, but most truly applicable to Lord Darnley.' In Hamlet's delay Shakespeare had in mind the backwardness of James to revenge his father's murder. 'Among other remarkable coincidences between the plot of Hamlet and the circumstances attendant on Mary and James, we may enumerate that of Dr. Wotton being sent into Scotland by Elizabeth as a spy upon James, and who afterwards entered into a conspiracy to deliver him into her hands.' Here we have the part of Rosencrantz and Guildenstern. 'The incident of Polonius being murdered in the presence of the Queen, in her closet, bears a resemblance to the murder of Rizzio in Mary's apartment.' 'Bothwell had poisoned Mary's cup of happiness, and it was her marriage with him that was the cause of her sorrows and death.'

"In 1797, Plumptre published an Appendix, in which additional parallelisms are given, and great stress is laid on the effects of poison on Darnley; Knox and Buchanan 'mention the black and putrid pustules which broke out all over his body;' this corresponds to the tetter, which 'bark'd about, most lazar like, with vile and loathesome crust, all the smooth body' of Hamlet's father. Hume's description of James (vol i, p. 1, 4, 4to ed,) is cited to show that the character of Hamlet is his character, 'but it is a flattering likeness; it is James drawn in the fairest colors; his harsh features softened and his deformities concealed.' Hamlet's love of the stage and patronage of the players resembled James's. Finally, from travellers' accounts, Plumptre infers that 'the shore on which Elsinore stands consists of ridges of sand, rising one above the other;' there could not, therefore, be any 'dreadful summit of a cliff that beetles o'er his base,' and 'looks so many fathoms down' amid such scenery; but this description suits Salisbury Crags and Holyrood Palace."

"This theory of Plumptre's (who, by the way, apologizes in his preface for any typographical errors to be found in the volume, on the ground of his excessive anxiety to publish his views before he could be anticipated and robbed of the glory of his discovery), this theory was treated with silent indifference for nigh three-quarters of a century, until a few years ago. It was revived in Germany, apparently without any suspicion that it was not novel. Carl Silberschlag, in the Morgenblatt, Nos 46, 47, 1860, brought forward the same arguments with which we are familiar to prove that under Gertrude was veiled an allusion to Mary Stuart, that Hamlet was James, and Claudius, Bothwell. But the ingenious German scholar went farther, and found that other characters in the tragedy had their prototypes among James's contemporaries. The laird of Gowrie had a father's murder to avenge, and had lived in Paris, and had a faithful servant named Rhynd, and met his death in an attempt by stratagem on the life of the King. All this prefigures Laertes and Reynaldo; unfortunately, an air of burlesque is cast over the theory by the argument gravely uttered, that Laird is pronounced just like (*ganz so klingt*) Laertes! After the death of the Laird, his bride, Anna Douglas, became insane,—hence Ophelia. In the 'vicious, mole' I, iv, 24, Silberschlag finds cumulative evidence of the truth of his theory." He identified it with James's congenital horror of a drawn dagger."

"Moberly noticed, though not in reference to this theory of Plumptre's, that the language with which Hamlet speaks of the dead body of Polonius is almost exactly the same as that used by the Porter at Holyrood in reference to the dead body of Rizzio. (See III, iv, 215)."

"Hunter (New Illustrations, etc. ii, 204) says if the composition of Hamlet can really be carried back to a time before 1589, 'there may be some ground for the opinion of those who have thought that there were strokes in it levelled at the Queen of Scots, who was put to death in 1587." In view of what has been advanced in these lectures there can be no doubt about the date being thus early.

It cannot be said that Plumptre presented his argument with much force. He was so enamoured of his idea that every possible suggestion seemed additional proof to him, and his zeal really injured his cause. Then no sufficient motive was suggested by him for the adoption of this play of Darnley's Murder by the author. Besides, much additional evidence has been brought to view since Plumptre's day, which throws light upon questions which could not be answered without it. The first known copy of Q 1 was only discovered in 1823, nearly a generation later, by Sir Henry Bunbury, and it is from the comparative study of this with Q 2 that some of the strongest proofs of this theory are derived. It has been so constantly asserted that the play of Hamlet was written by Shakespeare after 1597, and from ten to fifteen years later than its earliest production by some other author, that the points of resemblance in the murders have been disregarded by commentators. In 1597, Darnley's murder and Mary's execution were no longer in the arena of politics. There would be no political motive for selecting these incidents, or their analogue, as the basis of an appeal on the stage to king or people. But if the view be adopted that Shakespeare wrote the original acting-play of Hamlet in 1586 or 1587, most of the objections disappear to the theory that the plot pointed to the murder of Darnley and Mary's connivance in it, which were then on every tongue. Her execution was then the question of the day; his patrons were all personally deeply interested in the issue; all Europe was excited over it; and it was even used by Spain as a justification of the invasion of England by the Armada.

Am I right, then, in supposing that this play was originally intended to recall to memory the death of

Darnley, and to spur the timid James to connive at his mother's death, and perhaps even go beyond in pursuing his father's murderers? The Council may even have had in view the abhorrence of the Queen's death pretended by Elizabeth, whether it were real or disingenuous, and found in Hamlet, "the Encourager of Hesitancy." The three grounds for believing such the original intention of the tragedy should be first, the motives of the English Government and of Shakespeare himself in bringing out the play, which have been already perhaps sufficiently illustrated ; second, the resemblance in the plot and details of the play to the death of Darnley and the attendant circumstances ; and, lastly, the resemblance, shall I say identity, of the character of James I with that of Hamlet.

Furness' summary has given us Plumptre's argument in which the analogy of the plots is discussed, though somewhat hastily and heatedly. But I would ask the reader to follow me in this matter calmly. Let us look at the 'terrain.' Where is Hamlet located? German criticism thinks him into Germany. Dr. Eckardt (11 303), says: "Hamlet is a character of the North, where all life is more earnest and intense, etc." Bierne (11, 289) says: "Hamlet has a Northern soil, and a Northern heaven." Zimmermann (p. 341) says: "his character was found in the Danish world." And so with others. But all this is superficial. True, the play is of "Hamlet, prince of Denmark." But what did the word Denmark signify to Shakespeare? All his men are in reality British ; but they are veritably men, and hence all can, or may, comprehend them. To the German, they are Germans; to the Dane, Danes; to us, Americans. It is quite evident that Shakespeare knew nothing and cared nothing about Denmark—as such. His geography was of the most elastic kind. His Bohemia has a coast—an absolutely requisite one. But there is much to induce us to believe that if the word 'Scotland' was everywhere substituted for Denmark, and the whole pageantry were transposed from Elsinore to Edinburgh, we would have a graphic conception of the pictures that Shakespeare was making in his own mind, as he composed Hamlet. It is probable that Shakespeare visited Scotland in 1589 to play before the king; and the touches that characterize the locality may have been introduced after that period, though there is no good reason why he should not have learned about the topography before that from books and travellers. One of his patrons, Lord Hunsdon, had been on a mission to Scotland in 1584, and his son was also there in April, 1587, two months after Mary's death. The scenery is Scottish. The platform where Hamlet sees his father's ghost well describes Holyrood, the palace of James,—"the dreadful summit of a cliff that beetles o'er his base... and look so many fathoms down," but is entirely unlike Elsinore, which stand upon a series of sandy ridges.

We must bear in mind that there is nothing really medieval in the play, nor any attempt to conform it to the thought or customs of any former, much less a remote or barbarous, age. All is contemporaneous. The drunkenness and debauchery assigned to Denmark, which certainly did belong historically to

Hamlet's own barbarous era and country, were likewise the vices prevalent in Scotland. And, as the usurping Bothwell was one among the grossest examples of both vices in actual life, so Claudius, who fills his part in the play, is stigmatized throughout as the leader in all orgies. These assaults are put into the mouth of the Prince, the archetype of the youthful Solomon, who had not as yet displayed in full his taste for strong drink and other hereditary tendencies. He says satirically to Horatio, "We'll teach you to drink deep ere you depart." (1, 2, 175). Again,

> "The King doth wake to-night aud take his rouse,
> Keeps wassail, and the swaggering up-spring reels;
> And as he drains his draughts of Rhenish down,

etc. (1, 4, 10). "This heavy-headed revel", "they clepe us drunkards," "the bloat king," and many other similar expressions, are censures, which, though applicable enough to England then, still more forcibly point to Scotland and to Bothwell.

The Denmark of Shakespeare's Hamlet is not the Denmark of Saxo-Grammaticus, nor, indeed, of any other age or time. Lowell says *:

"In Hamlet, though there is no Denmark of the ninth century, Shakespeare has suggested the prevailing rudeness of manners quite enough for his purpose. We see it in the single combat of Hamlet's father with the elder Fortinbras, in the vulgar wassail of the king, in the English monarch being expected to hang Rosencrantz and Guildenstern out of hand, merely to oblige his cousin of Denmark, in Laertes, sent to Paris to be made a gentlemen of, becoming

'*Among my Books," p 208.

instantly capable of the most barbarous treachery to glut his vengeance." . . . "All through the play we get the notion of a state of society in which a savage society has disguised itself in the externals of civilization."

These remarks of Lowell, in his admirable essay on "*Shakespeare Once More*," are just, and, taken in connection with Shakespeare's method of appropriating what was at hand as the material into which he infused his vitalizing spirit, instead of hunting for it from afar, indicate that this Denmark of Hamlet was not only not a Denmark of the ninth century, but not Denmark at all, except in name. His spiritual Denmark was in the recesses of his own soul ; his fleshly Denmark was all about him. Nor had he far to go to find that which was at once sufficiently familiar for popular interest and yet remote enough for stage illusion. Scotland was near at hand ; Scotland was "a burning question ; " yet it was not trite or commonplace in London in the last quarter of the sixteenth century. And, measured even by such standard as the grossness of English manners, Scotland, in Shakespeare's day, offered a striking contrast, from its still ruder and more revolting forms of licentiousness, intemperance and cruelty, and invited the censure he affixes to the Court of Denmark. Courtiers could readily read between the lines. We have only to consult the writings of contemporaneous travellers to learn these facts.

Lowell says : "Shakespeare seems purposely to have dissociated his play from history by changing nearly every name in the original legend. The motive of the play—revenge as a religious duty—belongs only to a social state in which the traditions of barbarism are still operative; but with infallible artistic judgment Shakespeare had chosen, not untamed Nature, as he found it in history, but the period of transition, a period in which the times are always out of joint, and thus the irresolution which has its root in Hamlet's own character is stimulated by the very incompatibility of that legacy of vengeance he has inherited from the past with the new culture and refinement of which he is the representative."

Without intending it, Lowell has here described the exact social phase of Scotland, after the Reformation and before the Union, a veritable era of transition, and also the condition under which James found himself. He had been educated by his mother's bitterest enemies. Crafty and irresolute by nature, and trained in casuistry as well as in theology, his lot was cast in a time of religious and political revolution, a very "sea of troubles," with the personal legacy of revenge from a murdered father. How to acquit this debt was the question he had to meet. By punishment of the guilty, says the ghost, says his own first impulse, says the invisible chorus which seems to swell the symphony of revenge. By suicide, by submission, by delay, reply the timorous vacillating heart and the subtle speculative intellect. And while this debate defers decision, Fate steps in and mates the King, and sweeps from the board all the chief pieces in this game of life. And shall the real Prince, him of Scotland, take no lesson from all this?

Was it nothing to James that Hamlet, lamenting his father, cries out,

> "Yet I,
> A dull and muddy mettled rascal, peak,
> Like John-a-dreams, unpregnant of my cause,
> And can say nothing; no, not for a King,
> Upon whose property and most dear life
> A damned defeat was made."

Will it be believed that a plot so personal to him, with a moral so pointed and so applicable, was not intended for him, or that he took no note of it; and that, with his eager chase of questions of conscience, "motes to the mind's eye," it may not have weighed with him to soothe his scruples in patching up an alliance with the slayers of his mother? We know, as a fact, that while he professed a bitter indignation, he took no action, and accepted the fruits of the bloody deed. Doubtless many arguments commended themselves to him; peace, a pension, Protestantism; why not, too, as a case of conscience, the religious duty of revenge? "If thou hast nature in thee bear it not," says the Ghost.

I have now sketched out for you how this great drama most probably originated, with some of the resemblances of the plot to Darnley's murder. That the play had its source in a political pamphlet and grew to a world-poem does not at all militate against the theory. In my next and last lecture, I will endeavor to offer satisfactory evidence, as I believe, that Hamlet was at first drawn as a portrait of James VI. of Scotland.

THE PROTOTYPE OF HAMLET.

> "If we are like you in the rest, we will resemble you in that.
> *Merchant of Venice*, III., 1.
> "No counterfeit, but the true and perfect image of life, indeed.
> 1 *Henry IV.*, V., 4.

I have in my former lectures, I hope, made clear to the minds of my audience the powerful psychological insight with which Shakespeare revealed the dark places of a human soul, and that he was able to do so because it was with an actual human soul that he was dealing. I have laid before you some of my reasons for believing that I had discovered the individual men upon whose labyrinthine nature he had turned the focal light of his inquiry. In this lecture I will adduce further proofs to show that in this identification of the archetype, I was not mistaken.

Suppose we now take this matter *de novo*, unbiassed by any of the great authorities who have set out with theories to establish in regard to it. To begin at the beginning, Saxo Grammaticus, a writer of the twelfth century, gives a rough legend of one Amleth, who was in truth a historical character, regnant in Jutland, toward the close of the sixth century. Belleforest, a French writer, printed a version of this legend, about 1570, from which it is said a translation was soon afterwards made into English. Furness thus describes it : "This prose narrative is a bald, literal, and, in many respects, uncouth translation." The only copy extant was printed in 1608, but it is generally believed that the translation itself was made soon after the original book was printed 1570. Collier characterizes this production thus : (Ibid p. 88,) "It will be found that the tragedy varies in many important particulars from the novel, especially towards the conclusion ; that nearly the whole conduct of the story is different; that the catastrophe is totally dissimilar, and that the character of the hero in the prose narrative is utterly degraded below the rank he is entitled to take in the commencement. The murder of Hamlet's father, the marriage of his mother with the murderer, Hamlet's pretended madness, his interview with his mother, and his voyage to England, are nearly the only points in common." It is, indeed, ably contended by Elze, in which Furness agrees with him, that the prose history of Hamlet in English was of later date than the first sketch of the play. In my opinion, while this is true, at least of the version in the edition of 1608, it is not a matter of great consequence. The playwright, whoever he was, that conceived the first sketch of Hamlet, was after all indebted to the legend, in whatever form he learned it, for but the merest outline of the action and situations, nothing for the language, nothing for the characterization, nothing for the motive, the rational causes, that lead to the catastrophe. Capell says (p. 87) "It is rather strange that none of the relater's **expressions** have got into the play," except when

Hamlet cries out, "A rat, a rat," which is not in Belleforest, and was probably taken from the play, in the later editions of the translation. The same may be said of Hamlet's reproaches to his mother. In nought else does the diction of the two productions conform. Again, nothing could be more unlike than the characters. In the legend, the persons of the drama are vikings, who wade red-handed through blood, striking straight at the throats of their antagonists. Their stratagems are the clumsy ambuscades of half savage warriors. But this rude limning has been filled in by a master hand in the play, and is supplemented by the craftiest finesse in action and the subtlest speculation in thought. And so of the motive; in the legend, revenge and a throne are the stakes, and the action is a combat of broadswords and shields; in the tragedy, an intellectual mastery—a triumph in statecraft—seems the aim, waged by a practice of poisoned foils, a play of rapiers between masters of fence. It appears more than probable that some reader of Belleforest's French Chronicle, or perhaps of the English translation, had given an oral outline sketch of the legend of Hamlet to the playwright—the unknown playwright whom I have identified with Shakespeare, and who first called into being this unique work of genius.

Let us see how near the two stories approach each other. In the old legend, King Rorik of Denmark has a daughter, Geruth, or Gertrude, whom he marries to Horvendile, one of his "valiant, warlike lords." When Rorik dies, Horvendile becomes King, as is evident, in right of his wife, the Queen, heiress of

Rorik. His brother Fengon murders him, and he too, marrying the widow, becomes king by the same title, with the consent of the realm. It was by his marriage with Queen Mary that Darnley got his title, "King Henry"; and it was thus that his murderer, Bothwell, hoped to mount the throne.

It has always been a mooted question, both in the play and in Darnley's taking off, whether the Queen were an accessory before or after the fact; but certainly, in both cases, in a brief three months she married with the murderer. Indeed, the coincidence in time is significant. Hamlet cries out,

"Scarce two months dead, etc."

And again, "Look you how cheerfully my mother looks, and my father died within these two hours"; to whom Ophelia, "Nay, 'tis twice two months, my lord:" and in his Soliloquy (Act i, Sc. 2), "but two months dead, nay, not so much as two;" and yet again, "Nay, not a month." Darnley was assassinated, February 10th by Bothwell, who married Queen Mary, May 14th. Hamlet's expressions are intentionally extravagant; Ophelia's, deprecatory. Together, they emphasize the essential point, the indecent haste of the nuptials.

When we come to consider the death of Darnley, and the relations of Mary and Bothwell, we cannot fail to be struck by the wonderful similarity of the situations. Darnley, with all the intrinsic baseness of his nature, was yet a prince of royal lineage and one of the handsomest men of his time, and was especially noted for his splendid presence; he was nearly seven feet in height. Mary is said to have conceived a violent passion for him, which a short matrimonial experience converted into an intense hatred. It was not to the purpose of the poet to indicate how ill deserved was the love and how well merited was the hatred. But it was believed, whether true or not, that Mary's relations with Bothwell, before Darnley's death, were criminal. There can be no doubt that Bothwell murdered him, and that Mary married Bothwell scarcely three months thereafter. Her apologists alleged that her marriage was under duress; but the appearances, at least, were against her, and the marriage was in open day, and of its date we can have no doubt. The poet did not in Hamlet clearly define his view as to whether the Queen was an accomplice before the fact, or not. It was neither necessary nor prudent to enter on that discussion.

Shakespeare points to the beauty of the lawful husband, and the contrast with his murderer more than once:

> "See, what a grace was seated on his brow;
> Hyperion's curls, the front of Jove himself,
> An eye like Mars to threaten and command;
> A station like the herald Mercury
> New lighted on a heaven-kissing hill;
> A combination and a form indeed,
> Where every god did seem to set his seal,
> To give the world assurance of a man:
> This was your husband."
>
> "Look you now, what follows:
> Here is your husband, like a mildewed ear,
> Blasting his wholesome brother."

Hamlet in melancholy mood points the contrast,

"Hyperion to a satyr," which suggests the rugged adventurer who had murdered "King Henry"; and he recalls Mary's transient, yet doting, passion for Darnley:

> "Heaven and earth!
> Must I remember? Why she would hang on him,
> As if increase of appetite had grown
> By what it fed on; and yet within a month—"

And here may be noted the influence of the tenure of the royal title upon the mind of Hamlet, as conceived by Shakespeare and his contemporaries, which was quite different from the view taken of it by most of the commentators at the present day. It is now nearly always assumed that Claudius was a mere usurper, and that it was veriest imbecility in Hamlet to hesitate to strike down the wretch who had robbed him of his lawful inheritance. But such was not actually the case. In the legend, and presumably in the play, the Queen was as veritably sovereign as Victoria now is; and Hamlet had no rights while she lived. Claudius, too, as King-Consort, was the legitimate monarch. He styles Gertrude,

> "Our sometime sister now our queen,
> The imperial jointress to this warlike state." *

No note of insurrection, revolt, opposition, or even protest, is recorded of Hamlet, or the Court, or nation, against his accession.

---

* Schmidt's Shakespeare Lexicon defines "jointress" here as "a dowager", which is substantially the meaning; a jointure being an estate in lieu of dower. The idea involved is that she was sovereign of Denmark by right after her first husband's death, and not, as it is sometimes interpreted, joint-tenant, or sharer, of the throne with Claudius.

Inheritance of the throne by assent, as well as by consent, was not unknown to the English constitution. Indeed, assent is a tacit and implied consent, which was generally procured as the ratification, and not as the origin, of the title.

True, Hamlet calls Claudius,

> "A cut purse of the empire and the rule,
> That from a shelf the precious diadem stole
> And put it in his pocket. (III, 4, 100).

But this properly refers to the crime with which he paved his way to the throne, and which tainted a good title; just as Richard III.'s legitimate accession to the throne was vitiated by the murder of his nephews. Claudius announces Hamlet as his heir, and the courtier Rosencrantz considers his prospect for the succession "as advancement." There were many aspirants to the hand of Mary after the deaths of Darnley and Bothwell, and these all expected to share the throne with her.

With the transmission of the crown by royal bequest, the English Nation was also quite familiar. Henry VIII. was in the habit of giving it away by testament. Edward VI. also tried to do so. Elizabeth later confirmed James I.'s legitimate title by an alleged "dying voice." In the play, Hamlet exclaims :

"I cannot live to hear the news from England. But I do prophecy the election lights on Fortinbras : he has my dying voice." This is doubtless an implication of some suzerainty in England, but it points, at least, to the looseness of the hereditary principle in early English history, of which there were so many precedents; as, for instance, William Rufus,

Henry I., Stephen, John, Henry IV., Richard III. and Henry VII.

The title of Claudius to the throne was good enough, if it had not been based upon treason, adultery and murder. Hamlet was still heir-apparent to the throne, to which he could look forward also as "the most immediate to our throne," by the adoption and declaration of Claudius. It was a hard dilemma in which he was placed, for as the ghost could not be produced in court, to accuse Claudius of an improbable crime and there was no writ that ran into Purgatory, if Hamlet killed the king he would have stood convicted of quasi-parricide, and of regicide, and would have achieved infamy, instead of the crown. Werner, Corson, and others rely upon this to prove that Hamlet was not irresolute; but a resolute man is one who is equal to arduous occasions, not merely to easy ones.

This matter of regicide was "a living issue" at that day. The fall of kings and the mighty ones of earth was just then a common subject for men's thoughts, to which Sackville's grand poem had led the way. Macbeth and Lear and Shakespeare's historic cycle sound all the changes of the imperial theme. But here is a goodly king done to his death by the treasonable guile of a foul upstart, and his cherished wife consenting to the atrocious crime and raising the assassin to share her bed and throne. What should the princely heir in such case do, warned, or not, by visions from beyond the grave? His father's ghost bids him, "Revenge." His own faint heart holds him ever back. He is not to touch his mother's form, but to wring her heart.

Could he listen unmoved to the self-reproach of his own "counterfeit presentment," pointing out revenge as the path of duty?

> "How all occasions inform against me,
> And spur my dull revenge
> How stand I then,
> That have a father killed, a mother stained,
> Excitements of my reason and my blood,
> And let all sleep?
> O, from this time forth,
> My thoughts be bloody, or be nothing worth."

But if he refuses his mission, and inflict not justice upon the murderer, if he leave not the guilty queen to the vengeance of heaven, or her *enemies*, then— then—on him, on all, shall fall the wrath of an outraged deity, and the divine Nemesis will overwhelm the fated house in one universal wreck. The lesson of Hamlet is not against indecision in minor matters, but for boldness and resolution in the most momentous issues, and under the most difficult and trying circumstances. The object is not to exhibit the failure of a feeble will, but to show that Fate demands as an adversary whom she will respect a Will adequate to any possible human conditions. "Human fortitude should be equal to human adversity." It is hardly possible that such a lesson and warning would fall without effect either upon the Court or the injured prince:—and who was there to pity that most seeming guilty queen?

How much of Hamlet is James or portraiture, how

much Shakespeare or spiritual projection, it would be be hard to estimate. This was the age of dramatic incubation; and from the germ of that precocious Blood-Tragedy, "Hamlet, Revenge!", a political pamphlet in intention, grew an immortal poem. But it was the action, not the speculation which ten years later was introduced into it, that made it suddenly the target of envious rivals, a favorite at Court, and one of the author's chief stepping-stones to fortune and fame.

What could be more natural than that the son of murdered Darnley should stand as prototype for the son of murdered Denmark? And, if our surmise be correct, that the lesson was for James, what more effective way could be devised than to point the moral in the principal person of the Drama? But, in stating this hypothesis, I have been often met with the exclamation, "But how unlike are Hamlet and James in character!"; to which my reply is, "How like!" Let us see if this can be made good.

In looking at the character of James, we must not regard him with the eyes of Sir Walter Scott, who portrayed him in his debauched old age, nor even as he appeared to contemporaries after drunkenness and craft and cowardly cruelty and vicious indulgence had done their perfect work in him.

Scott follows Sir Antony Weldon, who thus describes him long after the date of Hamlet, and when he had become king of England.

"James I. was of a middle stature, more corpulent through (*i.e.*, by means of) his clothes than his body, yet fat enough. His legs were very weak, having had, as was thought, some foul play in his youth, or rather before he was born, so that he was not able to stand at seven years of age. That weakness made him ever leaning on other men's shoulders. His walk was ever circular."

We are reminded in this description of the allusion to Hamlet, by the Queen ; "He's fat and scant o' breath."

Scott, in the fortunes of Nigel, gives the following as his own estimate of James : " He was deeply learned, without possessing useful knowledge; sagacious in many individual cases, without having real wisdom ; fond of his power, and desirous to maintain and augment it, yet willing to resign the direction of that, and of himself, to the most unworthy favorites ; a big and bold asserter of his rights in words, yet one who tamely saw them trampled on in deeds ; a lover of negotiations, in which he was always outwitted ; and one who feared war, where conquest might have been easy. He was fond of his dignity, while he was perpetually degrading it by undue familiarity; capable of much public labor, yet often neglecting it for the meanest amusement; a wit, though a pedant ; and a scholar, though fond of the conversation of the ignorant and uneducated. Even his timidity of temper was not uniform ; and there were moments of his life, and those critical, in which he showed the spirit of his ancestors. He was laborious in trifles, and a trifler where serious labor was required ; devout in his sentiments, and yet too often profane in his language ; just and beneficent by nature, he yet gave way to the iniquities and oppression of others. He was penurious respecting money which he had to give from his own hand, yet inconsiderately and unboundedly profuse of that which he did not see. In a word, those good qualities which displayed themselves in particular cases and occasions, were not of a nature sufficiently firm and comprehensive to regulate his general conduct; and, showing themselves, as they occasionally did, only entitled James to the character bestowed on him by Sully—that he was the wisest fool in Christendom." (Fortunes of Nigel, Vol. 1, p. 89). This is James indeed, but it is not all of James. At this very period of his life, he was able to make a far more favorable impression on quick-witted and practiced diplomatists; and I can say this, though I hold the entire breed of Royal Stuarts in profound disgust.

Corvero, the Venetian Ambassador, in 1609, describes James I., then 43 years of age, as "of moderate height, of a very good complexion, of an agreeable presence, and of a very robust constitution, which he endeavors to preserve in its vigor. He ardently loves hunting, etc." "He knows how to exercise the art of reigning, and is endowed with an excellent understanding and extraordinary learning, having earnestly applied himself to study during his youth, but now he has entirely abandoned it." "He is very gentle, an enemy to cruelty, a lover of justice and full of good will." "He loves tranquillity, peace and repose; he has no inclination for war." (Rye's England as seen by Foreigners, pp. 229, 230). This vein of hatred of strife, except the war of words, runs all through the character of Hamlet.

Bishop Hackett, in his Life of Lord Keeper Williams (fol. 693, p. 38) says: "The King's (James I.) table was a trial of wits. The reading of some books before him was very frequent while he was at his repast. He was ever in chase after some disputable doubts, which he would wind and turn about with the most stabbing objections that ever I heard; and was as pleasant and fellow-like in all those discourses, as with his huntsmen in the field." (Idem, p. 277). This brings to mind Hamlet's wonderful word-play with Polonius and the courtiers, and with his dear friend Horatio.

I desire not to lay too much stress on minute resemblances, but one can scarcely help finding in these characterizations a likeness to Hamlet: "Sagacious in many individual cases, without having real wisdom," "a big and bold asserter of his rights in words, yet one who tamely saw them trampled on in deeds," "a lover of negotiations," "a wit though a pedant, and a scholar though fond of the conversation of the ignorant and uneducated," "even the timidity of his temper was not uniform, and there were moments of his life, and those critical, in which he showed the spirit of his ancestors."

Is not this the student from Wittenberg, scintillating, versatile, eloquent, infirm of purpose, jesting with fops and grave-diggers, who would not, or could not, put to the test his uncertain title to the throne, yet in a moment of supreme peril and agony executed dire vengeance on his murderous enemy, as did James, justly or unjustly, on Gowrie? But Shakespeare did not see James VI. of Scotland at twenty or even at thirty years old, as Scott saw him two centuries later. In their primy youth, all the Stuarts, mean as they were, had a certain beauty and glamour full of a promise which was as surely blasted by the secret canker of hereditary perfidy. James I. was not without it. A prig and a pedant doubtless he was, even before he came to man's estate, still the eyes of loyalty beheld in him a youthful Solomon. He was a student, well informed, one might say learned, fit to have been at Wittenberg, or elsewhere, with Hamlet, or as Hamlet. He wrote books. He had, too, a certain sort of wit of his own, compounded of drollery to the limit of buffoonery, word-dialectics, and a native shrewdness that was truly Scotch. Full of foolery, he was by no means a fool; and overflowing with sententious words of wisdom, he was yet the least wise of men. All the Stuarts, in a manner, realized the epigram on Charles II,

> "Whose word no man relies on,
> Who never said a foolish thing,
> And never did a wise one."

It will be remembered that James prided himself upon his "state-craft", by which he meant crooked counsels to compass infamous designs. His full-blown treachery was not as yet known of men, for in his youth he was only an apt neophyte in 16th century king-craft. But his foxy cunning and ready falsity were already cropping out. The Scotch Council knew him, Burleigh knew him, Elizabeth probably knew him; but, in the eyes of the great world, he was still the Heir Presumptive, the Coming Man. To courtiers, actors, authors, he appeared peaceable, not turbulent, gracious, fond of learning and literature, the patron of men of letters, a very Augustus but for his poverty, a prince held under a hard constraint of fortune by a rebellious nobility and the haughty domination of England. What a study he must have been to those psychologists, the politicians and the playwriters. What possibilities are in him, this sagacious stripling of twenty, intent to exalt and aggrandize his royal state, and yet so self-indulgent! And this vacillation of his—is it cowardly wavering and congenital faint-heartedness, the fruit of Rizzio's fatal ending, or is it the quintessence of a tortuous policy? Who shall say? But, whatever it be, it is the canker that threatens a brood of future ills to the state, the people, and the royal house. So much we may say now, looking backward, and so much may have been plain to a Maitland of Lethington, a Burleigh, a Walsingham, and even to the eye of the youthful seer, who read so truly the secrets of human hearts. To the young enthusiasts of England, James was indeed the Coming Man; and to a loyalist and conservative, such as Shakespeare, he might well stand for Ophelia's portrait of the Prince:

"The courtier's, soldier's, scholar's eye, tongue, sword.
The expectancy and rose of the fair state."

How great potentialities of good and evil lay enfolded in such a character. What prospects, expectations, predictions strewed his path. And it was, seeing these, that the tragedy proved to be a prophecy, instead of a warning, to the vacillating and fated house of Stuart.

"Such may be the character of James I," says the Hamlet-loving Shakespearian, "But surely you do not mean to compare the noble Dane to this perverse and crooked King, even when you make the best of him?" Bearing in mind that the James and the Hamlet of 1587 were not the same as a decade later, we may still answer, "yes!" The grand soliloquies belong to the Hamlet of 1597 not to the Hamlet of 1587: and, to paraphrase Dun Scotus, the difference between Scot and sot was, indeed, merely the interval between Prince and King. Much as Hamlet may enter into our secret moods, commend himself to our metaphysical introspection, and interest us in his personal fortunes, still he is just this creature that we have described James to be, only magnified by Shakespeare's loyalty, interpenetrated by Shakespeare's personality, and idealized by Shakespeare's genius. Shakespeare did not portray unmixed types, but men. It was because he had a man before his mind's eye, that in Hamlet he painted a man; and because this Hamlet is a man true to nature, that, in this truth to nature, he is full of subtle contradictions. This, indeed, it is that endows him with so profound an interest to us, because, in this waywardness of spirit, we see ourselves.

And just here may I be allowed to ask the question whether the creation of an ideal organic man in fiction,

> "One of the few, the immortal names
> That were not born to die,"

is possible without an actual archetype in real life? To me it seems that any particular effort by analysis and synthesis to build up an imaginary man must inevitably result in a puppet, or a Frankenstein, or, as the highest achievement of such art, in a literary picture or statue. Now, we all feel that there is in Shakespeare's characters, in Hamlet especially, who is now under our observation, something different from this. We feel that he is a real man, whose heart we see beating against his ribs, whose inarticulate sobs reach us, as well as his cries of protest against the disorder in the universe. Why is this so? We can lend ourselves easily enough to the illusion of the stage when it portrays the humors of men, under the masterly hand of Ben Jonson or Sheridan; but we know the difference. If Claudius were, indeed, "a king of shreds and patches," he would long ere this have been consigned to the lumber room. When Hamlet steps upon the stage, we feel that this is not mere acting. He is a resurrection, not a reconstruction. Under that inky robe a living spirit dwells. He is perennial, immortal, because he did once live. If an actual man had not stood as the pattern of that lofty dreamer, if Prince Hamlet were merely the coinage of the poet's brain, not the portraiture of an individual man, then long since he would have been but potsherds, the broken crystals of a vase, of which the intrinsic form was lost in pervasive space. If I am asked whether prototypes existed of Romeo, Falstaff, Hotspur, Shylock, Prospero, Lear, Macbeth, Othello, and all that goodly company, from whose actual, living lineaments the artist painted these wonderful portraits, I answer, 'yes.' Who they were I cannot now say, but I think I can tell you who stood with brooding brow, while Shakespeare drew "the dejected, 'havior of his visage." It was the young King James of Scotland, who has written in his tablets, "Remember thee ! Ay, thou poor ghost, while memory holds a seat in this distracted globe ; " and again, "O, most pernicious woman !", and last of all, "O villain, villain, smiling, damned villain !"

While I may not permit myself to be drawn aside into a too elaborate discussion of this question, I feel that an answer is due to those who shall object that artistic creation is the realization of an ideal, and not mere extrinsic photography. This is true ; but an ideal is not a conglomeration of qualities, or an adjustment of parts brought together from hither and yon ; it is essentially portraiture. For portraiture is the representation of an organism under the conditions in which it is viewed by the mind of the artist. We cannot say that the picture, or the dramatic character, is the absolute copy of the model. It is the semblance of the model as the artist beholds it, or as he chooses to behold it ; as it is, or as he feels it should be ; and as the first is his image of it, so the last is his ideal. But the ideal is but the image with something of the artist put into it ; a modification merely, not a complete creation, not a literary fabric. So, as I conceive Hamlet to have been written, Shakespeare made him, at first, perhaps altogether James, but, as his own soul and reason entered more and more into the contemplation and evolution of this favorite character, Hamlet grew in speculation, if not in character, with each touch, more like the player and less like the Prince, and hence nobler and grander ever.

If we do not assume Hamlet to be a perfect character, (being so like ourselves, as we all imagine), but take him up, and examine his record, as we may say, we shall discover more than ordinary blemishes, indeed acts that disclose radical defects. I am not disposed to take so extreme a view of the case as was propounded to me by a distinguished statesman of Kentucky. "My theory of Hamlet," said he, "is that he was a rascal, sir; a scoundrel, sir. He was a villain, and deserved the penitentiary, if, indeed, not the gallows. His treatment of Ophelia ought to have outlawed him. No gentleman would speak to a lady as he did, much less desert her as he did. Think, too, of that scoundrelly trick on Rosencrantz and Guildenstern. Would a man of honor put up a job like that? And as for his courage—why, the whole thing shows that he took it all out in talk. He wouldn't fight." This may be thought rather harsh judgment; but, certainly, in all of Hamlet's projects, plots, indirections, outbursts of rage, hesitations, quibblings with conscience, vengeance in words and wavering in deeds, profound philosophy and paltry action, we may find a likeness to the Royal Solomon. There are people who find Macbeth a modest gentleman, and Hamlet a heroic, resolute, direct man; but such is not the verdict of common-sense. His affectation of madness, his tortuous conduct with Ophelia, his conceit that "he play's the thing,

"Wherein I'll catch the conscience of the King," his counterplot, when "benetted round with villainies," for the destruction of Rosencrantz and Guildenstern, his determination to slay the King and his wasted opportunity, evince a faint heart, an unready hand and a wavering will. We seem to behold Gowrie entrapped and slain ; Sir Thomas Overbury perishing in prison, "between the pass and fell incensed points of mighty opposites ;" and Raleigh lingering in a dungeon and dying on the scaffold for too faithful service. Indeed, even in such minor details as his contempt for female love and his entire trust in his favorite Horatio, we may discover in Hamlet a likeness to James, who disliked women, neglected his queen, and lavished an overweening fondness on his male favorites.

A very strong contrast might be drawn, it is true, between the formality of James' mind, and the lofty imagination and profound speculation of Hamlet ; but it must be borne in mind that Buchanan—good schoolmaster, man of great talents,—made James, (what there was of him), and that Shakespeare made Hamlet. Shakespeare portrayed James as Hamlet ; but into that earthen vessel he threw the sublime light of his own genius until the vase becomes translucent as crystal. This is the endowment of genius. It is thus that the artist will paint Cæsar Borgia with a satanic beauty, and Milton will plant upon the brow of the foul fiend himself the majesty of an unconquerable pride.

There are some very striking evidences in the play itself confirmatory of the view that the prototype of Hamlet was a real person, not a fictitious one, and that this person was King James of Scotland. In the accepted version of the drama, based upon the Second Quarto, Hamlet is clearly stated to be thirty years old. In the grave-digger scene (Act. V. S. 1), occurs the following conversation:

> *Hamlet.* How long hast thou been a grave-maker?
> *First clown.* Of all the days in the year
> I came to't that day that our last
> King Hamlet o'ercame Fortinbras.
> *Hamlet.* How long is that since?
> *First clown.* Cannot you tell that? Every fool can tell that. It was *the very day* that young *Hamlet was born*.... I have been sexton here, man and boy, *thirty* years."

Hamlet recollected well, 'Poor Yorick,' whose "Skull now hath lain you, i' the earth three and twenty years," as the grave-digger tells us.

Hamlet says, "Alas, poor Yorick! I knew him, Horatio; a fellow of infinite jest, of most excellent fancy. He hath borne me on his back a thousand times, etc." This would suit very well the jester's play with a boy of six or seven. Since then three and twenty years have passed, and now he is thirty. This all seems sufficiently explicit, even if we neglect the Queen's comment on his fencing, "He's fat and scant of breath;" a sentence which, by-the-bye, does not occur in Q 1, as it would not have been true of James at twenty, when the first play was written. The prototype had grown stout, as well as ten years older, in the interim between the first cast of the play, and the last version. It seems evident, therefore, that, for some purpose, the poet fixes the age of Hamlet at thirty. If this play were revised, or, as we should rather say, rewritten, in 1596, as we have shown to be probable, Hamlet was then just the same age with James, who was born in 1566.

But to represent Hamlet as thirty years old creates a very serious discrepancy in the play, which the critics have not been able satisfactorily to account for. Blackstone says, "The poet in the fifth act had forgot what he wrote in the first." In all the earliest parts of the play, Hamlet appears to us, indeed, as in the first flower of youth. The very first allusion to him is as "young Hamlet."

Laertes (Act. 1, Sc. 3), speaks of Hamlet's love for Ophelia thus,

> "For Hamlet, and the trifling of his favor,
> Hold it a fashion, and a toy in blood,
> A violet in the *youth* of *primy* nature."

This toy in blood, *i.e.* caprice of impulse, this sweet flower of nature's springtime, has no proper reference to a man of thirty.

And Polonius says to her, (Act. 1, Sc. 3, v. 123),

> "For Lord Hamlet,
> Believe so much in him that he is *young*,
> And with a larger tether he may walk
> Than may be given to you."

This language is only applicable to early youth. Indeed, the critics agree, with few exceptions, that he was a youth, somewhere between 17 and 21 years of age. Richard Grant White puts him at twenty. He and his companions came back from the University of Wittenberg to attend his father's funeral, and he proposes to return. And, though it is urged by some who cannot deny the authenticity of the text, which makes him thirty, that students of that age may be found at the German Universities, yet such is not a princely custom now, and less so was it in Shakespeare's time, an age of strenuous action.

Furnivall says: "The two parts of the play are inconsistent on this main point in Hamlet's state." And Halliwell, to reconcile so patent a discrepancy, even ventures conjecturally (or arbitrarily rather), to alter the text from "thirty years" to "twenty," and from "twenty-three" to a "dozen years." In this last instance he follows the reading of the First Quarto, which embodied the earlier Hamlet, written ten years before the Revision, contained in the authorized version of Q 2. Such a change gives consistency to the action, though not to the character as developed in the Second Quarto, where Hamlet's introspection reveals a larger experience of life than belongs to early manhood. Besides, it is an unwarranted sacrifice of the text, which no critic has a right to make. Much of the language and action of Hamlet is explicable by supposing him a youth of twenty, which would be unworthy of a man of thirty. The whole tone of address to him by the King and Queen, combining authority and solicitude, seems to assume his youth and dependence, and to lack that implicit deference, which is almost instinctively paid to maturity, even in inferiors. Polonius patronizes him, and the easy approach of courtier friends reveals docility and lack of state. The reconciliation of these difficulties consists in constantly bearing in mind that Q 1 regarded a youth of twenty; and that in that earlier version everything is consistent with that view of him. But when the last Hamlet was written, the prototype had become a man of thirty, and this fact is so impressed upon the author's mind that he says so. But then his revision was chiefly by additions and interpolations in language and thought, and the changes of fact made were of very obvious points. The Second Quarto emphasizes the fact that Hamlet is thirty years of age, a fact unnecessary to the action; but it neglected to alter the by-play, the minor touches, which had in the earlier play pointed to and illustrated his youth. He was left a student, etc. It is as if a painter were to re-touch the portrait of a maiden, giving her the face of a matron, but leaving to her the dress of girlhood, and all the flowers of May. The explanation seems to be that in the earliest version he did have in view a youth of twenty, and so painted him; but when, a decade later, he re-wrote the play, as his hero—an actual man—had grown ten years older, he stated that fact, he made him thirty, he changed "the dozen years" since he was a little lad to "three and twenty;" but, with his customary play-house carelessness, he overlooked many touches which had marked his youth. In the First Quarto the grave-digger says:

"Looke you heres a skull hath bin here this dozen yeare."

In the later version he puts it:

"Here's a skull now hath lain you i' the earth three and twenty years."

"A dozen" is twelve, but it is not used to signify

exactness of time, except that it must have been so long, at least since Yorick was playfellow of the boy Hamlet. Now, in the Second Quarto, Hamlet is made thirty years of age, and this "dozen" is altered to "twenty-three," indicating that ten or eleven years had passed since that first draft of the play. In that lapse of time a real character would grow just so much older; but a fictitious character, the figment of the author's brain, or the creature of an old romance, would not have gained a day in age. In the mind of his creator, to him would belong a perennial youth. Oliver Twist is always young; the fat boy is a boy still. From this it appears that whoever might be the prototype of Hamlet, he must have been a real person at least, whether James or some other; and the only question is whether any other was more likely than James to be such prototype.

In the First Quarto, in the Interlude, the Player King opens his speech to the Queen with the words:

> "Full forty years have passed, their date is gone,
> Since happy time joined both our hearts as one, etc."

The "forty years" have here no special significance, except to indicate the special atrocity of the murder. But in the Second Quarto, the King's speech is altered, and lines inferior in melody and vigor, but more explicit, are substituted:

> "Full *thirty* times hath Phœbus' cart gone round
> Neptune's salt wash and Tellus' orbed ground;
> And *thirty dozen moons*, with borrowed sheen,
> About the world have times twelve thirties been,
> Since love our hearts and Hymen did our hands
> Unite, commutual in most sacred bands."

Why this change? Is it not evident that it is to conform in general terms to the age assigned to Hamlet by the Grave-digger, to his thirty years when the play was recast!

When Shakespeare made this play, notable people sat for their portraits, and, when the gallery was finished, many had been the touch by which he had transformed the evanescent figures of the Court into immortals, beings more real, more historical than the originals. I have read a good deal of criticism on Hamlet, but nowhere have I seen the character of Polonius better portrayed than by Goethe. The gift of genius, insight, seeing through shams the "naked frailties" of the soul, enabled him to account this typical courtier at his true value. It is this gift, which at a later day so endeared the large-hearted Thackeray to us. Shakespeare meant to portray some particular personage when he put Polonius on the the stage. Who was this grave and reverend chamberlain, with his wise saws, his apt allusions, his worldly wisdom and his spiritual blindness? Here is a problem not yet solved. Was it Burleigh or Sir Nicholas Throckmorton, or some lesser wight, who had offended the players or their patron? Who can tell? When a consensus of critics accepts James as Hamlet, I will unriddle the rest of it. Wilhelm Meister loquitur:

"I engage," said he, " on this occasion, to present a meritorious person in his best aspect. The repose and security of this old gentleman, his emptiness and his significance, his exterior gracefulness and interior meanness, his frankness and sycophancy, his sincere roguery and deceitful truth, I will introduce with all due elegance in their fit proportions. This respectable, gray-haired, enduring, time-serving knave, I will represent in the most courtly style; the occasional roughness and coarseness of our author's strokes will further me here. I will speak like a book when I am prepared beforehand, and like an ass when I utter the overflowings of my heart. I will be insipid and absurd enough to chime in with everyone, and acute enough never to observe when people make a mock of me. I have seldom taken up a part with so much zeal and roguishness."

Wilhelm had also allowed both Rosencrantz and Guildenstern to continue in his play. "Why not compress them into one?" said Serlo. "This abbreviation will not cost you much."

"Heaven keep me from all such curtailments!" answered Wilhelm: "They destroy at once the sense and the effect. What these two persons are, and do, it is impossible to represent by one. In such small matters we discover Shakespeare's greatness. These soft approaches, this smirking and bowing, this assenting, wheedling, flattering, this whisking agility, this wagging of the tail, this allness and emptiness, this legal knavery, this ineptitude and insipidity,— how can they be expressed by a single man? There ought to be at least a dozen of these people, if they could be had; for it is only in society that they are anything; they are society itself; and Shakespeare showed no little wisdom and discernment in bringing in a pair of them. Besides,

I need them as a couple that may be contrasted with the single, noble, excellent Horatio."

When Bothwell was captured in 1567, he was taken before Eric Rosencrantz, Governor of Bergen, who sent him to the king of Denmark. In 1576 Bothwell died in prison in Denmark, and Mary and her friends claimed that he made a confession, exculpating her from all share in her husband's murder. The genuineness of the confession was denied, and Mary prayed that an appeal be made to the witnesses, among whom was one "M. Gullanstarn," as she spelt it. The coincidence with the Rosencrantz and Guildenstern of Hamlet is curious. The latter name, though of the ancient nobility, has often been dishonored.

Shakespeare did not neglect another aspect of the courtier in Osric; and even Laertes presented features often seen in the train of "Good Queen Bess."

Too much stress ought not, perhaps, to be laid upon Ophelia's eulogy of "the beauteous Majesty of Denmark," a proper tribute to Queen Mary in 1586, at forty-four, and still more so at the time of Darnley's murder, but a strained compliment to the mother of a man of thirty, whose over-ripe charms would scarcely have stirred to fratricide "that adulterate beast," who seemed to have sought, through guilt, the woman as much as the Queen.

Froude says of her in regard to Babington's Conspiracy: "She was the old Mary Stuart still, the same bold, restless, unscrupulous, ambitious woman, and burning with the same passions, among which, revenge stood out prominent. Hers was the panther's nature— graceful, beautiful, malignant, untamable. What was to be done with her?" Perhaps, we ought all to thank God that she has been dead so many centuries before we were born, and pray to God that there may be few left like her.

It has seemed to me (am I led by the phantom of the Scottish sorceress?) that in the Play of Hamlet not enough is made of the Queen. She was one to breed all evil passions in the heart of man, and to gild them with the fascination of an irresistible beauty, an architect of ruin, a sure guide to moral anarchy. To me she seems portrayed in Swinburne's apostrophe to Queen Mary:

> "Love hangs like light about your name,
>   As music round the shell;
> No heart can take of you a tame
>   Farewell.
>
> Yet when your very face was seen,
>   Ill gifts were yours for giving:
> Love gat strange guerdons of my queen
>   When living.
>
> O diamond heart, unflawed and clear,
>   The whole world's crowning jewel!
> Was ever heart so deadly dear,
>   So cruel?"

Problems are sometimes started which are not easy to solve. On the theory that the vizard of Hamlet covered the face of James, a latent threat seems suggested in Fortinbras' claim, that he had "some rights of memory to this Kingdome." What princely soldier, "fresh from conquest," might answer to this young hero's unchallenged usurpation? Could it be Essex? Hardly in 1586–7, though the phrase may have come into the play at a later day. Could it be a covert compliment to the plausible and poisonous Leicester, who posed as patron of Puritan and play-actor alike ? Have Hamlet's dying words any significance in them beyond the sound?

> "I cannot live to hear the news from *England;*
> But I do prophecy the election lights
> On Fortinbras : he has my dying voice."

If the royal line failed, it was England which would settle the succession on a prince alien to Denmark, i.e. to Scotland. However, both England and Scotland were full of Pretenders with small pretense of title.

Now, then, let us go back for a moment, and see how this matter stands. In the years 1586 and 1587 there existed a strong motive on the part of the English Government to foment hatred against the name and memory of Mary, Queen of Scots. The hostility of the Government was but a reflection of the national feeling which was intense. It was also necessary to embitter the antagonism of James VI. of Scotland against his mother as much as possible. All the arts of diplomacy were employed for this purpose ; spies, go-betweens, subsidies, bribery, and whatever fear or flattery or favor could accomplish. It has frequently been a device of courts to utilize the stage to accentuate political action. The stage at that particular period was largely used to enforce personal views and to gratify personal ends. Now, at this critical moment, a play appears with a plot picked up apparently by accident, but with strikingly similar points to the murder of Darnley.

It is laid at the Court of Denmark, but all the drapery is more Scotch than Danish. The scenery is of Edinburgh, not Elsinore. The drunkenness and debauchery might attach to one as well as the other. The character of the usurping Claudius might well have been drawn from that of the ruthless and audacious Bothwell. And numerous allusions go to establish the essential identity of the plots of Hamlet with Darnley's murder. But, in addition to all this, James and Hamlet possess, with all their superficial differences, remarkable and radical points of resemblance in character. I have endeavored to show that Hamlet must be the likeness of a real man. When "Hamlet" was first written, in 1586, he was twenty years old, and so was James; when James reached thirty, the play was rewritten, and, lo! Hamlet had become thirty also. The curious circumstance that he keeps step in years with James corroborates the probability that it was James who sat for the portrait of Hamlet.

We find Shakespeare employing Hamlet as his mouthpiece, his oracle, the *vates* into whom he has breathed his divine afflatus. Hamlet utters his choicest thoughts, his profoundest suspirations, his most perplexed problems of life. But, surely, he did not intend to reveal himself fully therein. He propounds the riddle, but he does not even hint his own guess of its meaning. He is speaking, but it is through another; and what more exalted spokesman or interpreter could he select than his future King. "I am but a player," he says to his soul, "but my thoughts are royal thoughts; my winged words, heaven-born and heaven directed, befit the lips of a king." So that, according to my view, we have the poet, like an Apollo, standing invisible by the side of his Pythoness, who utters the voice of inspiration in sentences, pregnant though obscure. The body of Hamlet is James, but the Divinity who guides the motions of his soul is Shakespeare.

THE END.

INDEX.

A

Abbott's Shakespearian Grammar, 31.
Academical Study of Shakespeare, 29.
Action in Hamlet, The, 78–9, 99, 102, 152, 158.
Actors, their status, 146–7, 168.
Age of transition, 188–9, 190.
Algebra of the spirit, 53 to 60.
Amiel's Journal, 95–6–7–8.
Among my books, 188–9, 190.
Analysis of Hamlet. (See Hamlet.)
Anne Hathaway, 74.
Antony and Cleopatra, 31.
Apology for quotations, 105.
Arch of Gervinus, 38.
Assassination, 50, 169, 178.
Atheneum, Letter in, 51.
Attorney's clerk. (See Shakespeare, a Noverint.)

B

Bacon, Genius of Lord, 73.
Baconian paradox, 72–3, 124, 142–3–4, 160.
Banquo, 49, 50, 55, 57, 58, 59, 63, 66.
Beauties of Shakespeare, 44.
'Beauteous majesty of Denmark,' 181, 219.
'Beautified,' 128.
Belleforest, 179, 194.
Bierne, 186.
Biographies of Shakespeare's contemporaries, 135 to 139, 146–7–8.

Bishop Butler, 164.
Benedix, 91.
Blackstone, Sir Wm., 213.
'Bloody,' 58.
'Blood-boltered,' 58.
Bluntness of Macbeth, 61-2-3.
Bodenstadt, 58.
Booth, Edwin, 103.
Bothwell, 178, 181-2, 188, 195-6, 219, 222.
Boucicault, Dion, 72.
Brown, Charles Armitage, 117.
Buchanan, Geo., 211.
Bullen, 137.
Bunbury, Sir Henry, 185.
Burbage, 140, 151.
Burger's Macbeth, 57.
Burleigh, Lord, 169, 171, 176, 179, 205-6, 217.

C

Campbell, T., 45.
Campbell, Lord, 127, 134, 144, 166, 175.
Capell, 193.
Canons of dramatic construction, 37, 38, 55, 99, 100, 152.
Carey, Sir Robert, 173.
Cartwright, Robert, 144-5.
Central idea of drama, 37, 55-6.
Charles II., 205.
Chateaubriand, 91.
Chauteauneuf, 170.
Chettle, 128.
Chivalry, 30.
Chronicle Plays, 30.
Cibber, Colley, 91.
Clarendon Editors, 26, 31, 107-8-9, 115, 117-8, 157, 177.

INDEX.

Claudius, 84, 181, 183, 188, 194, 197–8–9, 222.
Coleridge, Hartley, 146-7.
Coleridge, Samuel T., 43, 75-6-7, 91, 102.
Collaboration, 115, 123, 135, 153.
Collier, 120, 193.
Comedy of Errors, 108.
Commentators, their dogmatism, 25, 28, 160-1.
Comparison with Bacon, 73-4.
Conscience, 61.
Contagion of crime, 59, 63, 65, 70.
Contagion of weakness, 87, 95, 98.
Contemptuous biography, 143, 146.
Contemporary excellence, 124, 134-5-6-7-8-9.
Contemporaries, their obscurity, 123, 136, 146-7.
"Conversations in a Studio," 56-7, 85, 155-6.
Coriolanus, 31.
Corson, 199.
Courtiers, 168, 179.
Corvero, 203.
Craik's English of Shakespeare, 31, 36.
Crime, Macbeth's, 50.
Crisis of Hamlet, 87.
Crisis of tragedy, 38-9.
Critical ineptitude, 56-7, 67, 91-2.
Criticism, Erroneous methods, 85, 124, 130-1, 136, 143, 160-1.
Criticism, Foreign (See Goethe and Werder, also), 56-7, 67, 85, 89, 90, 91-2, 175, 183-4, 186-7.
Culture, 41.

D

Darnley, Murder of, 173-4-5, 178 to 185, 191, 195-6-7-8.

Dates. (See Hamlet.)
Davies, Sir John, 149.
Davison, Secretary, 170, 176.
Delius, 117.
Delusion of sin, 62, 68, 70.
Disuse of Quarto First, 109–110.
Denmark, Shakespeare's, 186 to 190, 222.
Devonshire Hamlet's, 116.
Decisiveness, Hamlet's, asserted, 83-4, 90, 199.
Defects in plot of Hamlet, 79, 152.
Derby, Lord, 161.
Derby's Iliad, 42.
Destructive criticism, 124, 130, 160.
Dilemma, Hamlet's, 199.
Disappointment, Shakespeare's, 148.
Dogmatism of commentators, 24, 28, 160-1.
Drake, 45.
Drama, The Elizabethan, 20, 43-4.
Drama, its poetic basis, 102.
Drama, Founder of the Romantic, 134 to 139, 151-2.
Dramatic epic, 46.
Dramatic fecundity, 176.
Dramatic unities, 37 to 40, 98-9, 152.
Dregs of sin, 148.
Drunkenness and debauchery, 187 to 190, 222.
Drury, Sir Wm., 178.
Duncan, 49, 50, 57-8, 60, 63-4, 66.
Dyce, 121.

E

Early authorship of Shakespeare, 115 to 144, 150, 176-7-8.
Eckardt, 186.
Edward II, 173
Elements of genius, 131-2-3, 150.

INDEX.

Elsmere, Robert, 95.
Elsinore, 183, 187, 222.
Elze, 107, 125, 130, 193.
Elizabeth, Queen, 160, 162-3-4, 167, 169, 170, 177.
Elizabeth's court, 151, 168.
Elizabeth's council, 167, 169, 170-1-2-3, 176-7-8, 186.
Elizabethan age, 53-4-5-6, 163-4, 167-8-9.
Elizabethan drama, 20-1, 43-4.
Elizabethan dramatists, 43, 124, 134 to 139, 146-7-8, 176, 186.
'Encourager of hesitancy,' 186.
Energy a test of genius, 131-2-3, 150.
Energy of Shakespeare's times, 163.
English nationality, 163, 164.
'English of Shakespeare,' 31, 36.
Epic tragedy, Macbeth, 46.
Essex, 171, 182, 220.
Esthetic value of Shakespearian study, 22-3, 29.
Ethical value of Shakespearian study, 29.
Evil, Problem of, 58-9, 60.
Euphuism, 125.

F

'Fat and scant of breath,' 212.
Fate and Free Will, 48, 59, 79, 82-3, 88, 91-2-3-4, 99, 100, 157, 165, 190, 200.
Faust, 93.
Ficklen, Prof. John R., 20.
Final touches to Hamlet, 109, 112, 157-8-9.
First Folio, 26-7-8-9, 106.
First Quarto, 107 to 112, 116, 119, 175-6, 185.
First words of Macbeth, 55.
Fleay, 113, 115-16, 121-2, 126, 135-6, 140.
Folklore, 54.

Footsteps of Shakespeare, The, 144.
Fortier, Prof. A., 20.
Fortinbras, 220-1.
'Fortunes of Nigel,' 202-3.
Free Will. (See Fate and Free Will.)
Freiligrath, 90.
French critics, 91-2.
Froude, J. A., 34, 91, 170, 219.
'Frozen Toe, The,' 89.
Furness, Variorum, Hamlet, 26, 89, 180 to 186, 193.
Furnivall, 214.

G

Genius, Elements of, 131-2-3, 150.
Genius, Inspiration of, 102.
Genius, Precocity of, 140-1-2, 176-7.
Geography, Ideal, 187.
German critics. (See Goethe and Werder.) 56-7, 67, 85, 89, 90-1, 175, 183-4, 186-7.
'Germany in Hamlet,' 90.
Gertrude. (See The Queen.)
Gervinus, 45, 117.
Gervinus' arch, 38.
Globe Company, 140.
Gowrie, Earl, 52.
Gravedigger, The, 212, 215.
Greene (Dramatist), 122, 126-7-8-9, 135, 151.
Greene (Actor), 140.
Gerald Griffin, 141.
Goethe's inspirations from Shakespeare, 75-6-7.
Goethe's interpretation of Hamlet, 79, 80-1-2-3, 93, 98.
Goethe's "Polonius," 217.
Goethe's "Rosencrantz and Guildenstern," 218.
Gonzago Play, The, 85, 121, 145, 216.
Guildenstern, 179, 182, 189, 218-9.

"Groat's-worth of Wit, The," 128.
Gunpowder Plot, 53.

H

Hackett, Bishop, 204.
Hallam, 45.
Halliwell, 26, 113, 122, 138, 143, 214.
HAMLET THE PLAY.
  Alterations by critics, 91-2.
  Fate and Free Will, 48, 79, 82-3, 88, 92 to 100, 157, 165, 190, 200.
  Gonzaga Play, The, 85, 120-1-2, 145, 216.
  Hamlet, The First.
    Author, 112 to 119, 120 to 123, 130-1, 135 to 139, 142, 152, 177.
    Its date, 112, 115, 125 to 130, 140-1, 145, 169, 185.
    Notices, 112-13, 126 to 129, 152-3-4, 178.
    "Hamlet Revenge!" 129, 151, 177.
  Hamlet of Quarto First, 107-8, 110-11-12, 116, 119, 175-6, 185.
  Last Hamlet, The, 106 to 109, 111-12, 116, 119, 125, 152 to 159.
  Lesson of Hamlet, 82-3, 87-8, 93 to 104, 182, 190.
  Method of production, 151-2-3-4.
  Motives for production, 162-3, 166, 171, 173-4, 178.
  Origin, 116, 123, 142, 151 to 154, 161, 173-4, 178-9, 180, 192-3.
  Paragon of Plays, The, 37, 45, 78-9, 152.
  Parallel with Macbeth, 48, 78-9, 87, 94-5.
  Parallelisms to Darnley's murder, 173-4-5, 178 to 185, 191, 195 to 198.
  Plot, Crisis of, 99.
  Plot, Development of, 48, 151 to 158, 162.
  Plot, Rudeness of, 79, 152.
  Portraitures in play, 100 to 104, 183, 201 to 207, 209 to 211, 222-3.
  Queen as accessary, 181, 185, 195-6-7.
  Revenge as a duty, 173, 188-9-190-1, 199-200.
  Scene of action, 186, 190.
  Shakespeare's personality in Hamlet, 100 to 103, 154 to 158, 165.
  Significance, Theories of its.
    Author, 94.
    Coleridge, 85-6-7.
    French critics, 91-2.
    German critics, 85, 89-90-1.
    Goethe, 79 to 83, 85.
    Lowell, 87-8, 188-9-90.
    "No Philosopher," 101.
    Plumptre, 180 to 186.
    Werder, 83-4.
  Value as an acting play, 78-9, 99, 102, 152, 158.
HAMLET THE PRINCE.
  Character.
    Alleged madness, 92-3, 111.
    Craft, 81, 210-11.
    Indecision, 48, 80 to 88, 93 to 104, 199, 200.
    Introspection, 86 to 89, 94 to 100, 154-5.
    Learning, 80.
    Melancholy, 100, 154-5-6.
    Pessimism, 154 to 158.
    Skepticism, 100.
    Self-reproach, 101-2, 191.
    Word-Play, 179.
  Characterizations.
    Amiel, 95 to 98.
    Coleridge, 85 to 87.
    Goethe, 80-1-2-3.
    German critics, 89, 90-1.
    Kentucky critic, 210.
    Lowell, 87-8.

As an exponent of Shakespeare, 100 to 103, 154 to 158, 165.
Hamlet, a portrait, 101, 103-4.
Likeness to James I, 183, 201 to 207, 209-10-11, 222-3.
Mirror of all mankind, 101, 157-8-9.
Organic unity of character, 98, 99, 100-1-2.
Hamnet Shakespeare, 119, 125, 130, 156-7-8.
Hardihood of Macbeth, 60, 69.
Hazlitt, 26, 100, 103.
Heard, F. F., 127, 144.
Henry IV., 118.
Henry VI., 108, 119, 128.
Henry VIII., 30.
Henslow's Diary, 129.
Hero and Leander, 136.
Heroic drama, Macbeth, 46.
Hesitation. (See Indecision.)
Hieronymo, 121.
Histoires tragiques, 179.
Historical plays, The, 30 to 37.
Holinshed, 49, 66.
Holyrood, 183-4, 187.
How to study Shakespeare. (See Lecture I.)
Hudson, 26, 40.
Hume, David, 183.
Hunsdon, Lord, 170-1, 176, 179.
Hunter (New Illustrations), 184.
Hypostasis of Thor, 89.
"Hystorie of Hamblet," 179.

I

Ideals, Creation of, 207-8-9.
Impotence of man, 82. (See Fate.)
Incorrect notion of genius, 121-2-3.
Indecision of Hamlet, 48, 80 to 88, 93 to 104, 199-200.
Inhibition of 1597, The, 109, 112, 119.
"Innovation, The late," 109.

Interlude, The, 216.
Introspection, 86 to 89, 94 to 100, 154-5.
"Isle of Dogs," 109.
Isolation of Guilt, 70-1.

J

JAMES I.
Craft, 190.
Fondness for theatre, 173, 183.
Hume's character of James I., 183.
Indecision, 172, 182, 185, 190-1.
James in 1586-7, 171-2, 179, 190-1.
Likeness to Hamlet, 183, 201-2-3-4-5-6-7, 209, 210-11, 222-3.
"Joannes Factotum," 127-8.
Johnson, Dr. Sam., 25, 140.
"Jointress," its meaning, 197.
Jonson, Ben, 139, 142, 147-8.
Joy of life, 155.
Julius Cæsar, 31 to 37.

K

Karpf, C., 89.
Kenney, 100.
Kentucky theory of Hamlet, 210.
Keynote in first words, 55.
Keynote of Hamlet, 82-3, 93 to 104, 157, 182, 190.
Keynote of Macbeth, 55-6.
Kreyssig, 100.
"Kind Hart's Dream," 128.
King John, 30, 118, 158.
King Lear, 37, 46, 78, 91-2.
Knight, Charles, 40, 111, 117.
"Know Thyself!" 41.
Kyd, Thomas, 120-1-2-3, 135, 138, 139, 151.

L

Lady Macbeth, 44, 60, 63 to 69.
Laertes, 184, 188, 213, 219.

"Legal acquirements of Shakespeare," 127, 144.
Legend of Hamlet, 178–9, 188, 192–3–4.
Legend of Macbeth, 49–50.
Leicester, Lord, 170–1, 176, 221.
Leo's criticism, 67.
Lesson of Hamlet, 82–3, 87–8, 93–4–5, 98, 100 to 104, 190.
Lesson of Macbeth, 53, 71, 82–3.
Literary aspiration, 19, 20.
Literary collaboration, 115; 123, 125.
Literary education, 128–9.
Literature; its definition, 19–20.
Literature; its quickening power, 19, 20–1–2, 42.
Literature to be studied in literature, 24, 34.
Lodge, 129, 134.
Lost Soul, A, 71.
Love of evil, 50.
"Love's Labor's Lost," 118–9, 122.
"Love's Labor's Won," 119.
Lowell, Jas. Russell, 40, 87–8, 188–9–90.
Lowndes, 121.
Loyal zeal, 155, 165–6.
Lyly, 124, 135, 136, 139, 151.
Lyric power of Macbeth, 46.

M

MACBETH (Lecture 2d), 41 to 71.
 Burger's unconscious travesty, 57.
 Character of Macbeth, 61–2–3, 65, 69–70.
 Complement of Hamlet, 48, 94–5.
 Dramatis Personæ. (See Lady Macbeth, Duncan, etc.)
 Estimates of the play, 40, 45–6.
 Grandeur, Its, 37, 47, 78.
 Incompleteness, 45.
 Keynote, 55–6–7, 94–5.

Lyric movement, 55–6.
Moral lesson, 39, 53–4–5, 65, 69–70–1.
Parallel with Hamlet, 48, 94–5.
Plot, 49, 50–1–2.
Remorse of Lady Macbeth, 44, 60, 63, 69.
Remorse of Macbeth, 69–70.
Reticence of Macbeth, 61–2.
Scotland of Macbeth, 51–2.
Shakespeare's greatest poem, 45–6–7–8.
Mad, Was Hamlet? 92–3, 111.
Madness, 93.
Malone, 120, 144.
Man, the greatest mystery, 94.
Marlowe, Christopher, 115–6, 123, 128, 135 to 139, 142, 156, 173.
Mary, Queen of Scots, 160 to 191. (See also James I., Darnley and Bothwell.)
 Apostrophe by Swinburne, 220.
 An accessory to Darnley's murder, 181, 185, 195–6–7.
 English hatred and machinations, 169 to 176.
 Execution, 175, 185.
 Fascination, 220.
 Innuendoes of Sh.? 180–1, 184.
 Marriage to Bothwell, 178–9, 181–2.
 Master of Grey's letter, 172–3.
 Murder of Darnley, 173–4–5, 178–9, 181, 191.
 Political intrigues, 169 to 176.
 Plumptre's argument, 174, 180 to 184.
Masque, The, 122.
Massinger, Life of, 146.
Master of Grey, 172–3.
Menaphon, Greene's, 126.
Merchant of Venice, 37, 118.
Meres, Francis, 118–9–20, 130, 149.

INDEX.

Metaphysics of Shakespeare, 156, 165.
Method of Composition, 151-2-3.
Method of study, 31 to 37.
"Midsummer Night's Dream," 108, 122, 178, 180.
Milton, 141.
Milton on Shakespeare, 133.
Milton's Satan, 58.
Mirror of all mankind, The, 158-9.
Mixed metaphor, Goethe's, 76.
Moberly, 184.
Moral culture of the drama, 20, 43-4.
Moral of Macbeth, 39, 53-4-5, 65, 69-70-1.
Moral proportion, Sense of, 38-9.
Motives for producing Hamlet, 162-3, 166, 171 to 178.
"Much Ado About Nothing," 108.
Murder of Duncan, 45, 63.
"Mystery of Hamlet, The," 161.
Mythology, 54.

N

Nash, Thomas, 109, 125-6-7, 129, 135, 138, 139.
National progress, 30, 163-4.
"Neckverse, To latinize their," 126.
Nemesis, 39, 48, 58, 69-70-1, 179, 200.
"No Philosopher," 101.
Norman mind, The, 164.
Noverint, The, 126-7, 129, 130, 144-5, 151.

O

Odium theologicum, 160.
Opportunity, 131, 151.
Original design of Hamlet un-ambitious, 142, 152-3, 161, 178.
Osric, 219.
Othello, 37, 45-6, 78.
Ownership of plays, 106, 109-110, 152-3.

P

Paradox, Werder's, 83-4, 90, 199.
Paragon, Hamlet, The, 37, 45, 78-79, 152.
Parallel between Bacon and Shakespeare, 73-4.
Parallel between Hamlet and Macbeth, 48, 78-9, 87, 94-5.
Parallel between Shakespeare and Marlowe, 137-8-9.
Parallel between Shakespeare and Plutarch, 33.
Parallelisms between Hamlet and Darnley's murder, 173-4-5, 178 to 185, 191, 195 to 198.
Patriotism of the English, 164-5, 174-5.
Patriotism of Shakespeare, 158-9, 165, 167-8.
Patronage, 127, 167-8, 170-1.
Peccavi, 104, 157.
Peele, 135-6, 139.
Pericles, 118-9, 144-5.
Permanence of Shakespeare's influence, 22, 124, 149, 159.
Persons of the drama, 91.
Pessimism, 154-5-6-7.
Perturbed spirit, The, 157-8-9.
Play actors, their standing, 167-8.
Play within a play, 85, 121-2, 145, 216.
Plays as political devices, 168, 173-4, 176-7-8.
Players, Companies of, 109, 140, 170.
Player King, The, 216.
Plots, common property, 123.

INDEX.

Plot of Hamlet, 79, 99, 151 to 154, 161, 173-4, 179, 193-4-5.
Plot of Macbeth, 49-50.
Plots against Elizabeth, 160.
Plots against James I., 52-3.
Plumptre, Rev. James, 180 to 186.
Plutarch and Shakespeare, 33.
Poetry the basis of the drama, 102.
Poet's function is representation, 93-4.
Politics, Elizabethan, 164, 168 to 179.
Polonius, 179, 182, 184, 213, 217-8.
Portraiture in Hamlet, 97, 100-1-2-3-4, 157-8, 200-1, 207 to 217.
Præ-Shakespearian Hamlet, 114-5, 123.
Precocious genius of Shakespeare, 44, 114 to 142, 154 to 158, 176-7.
Precocity of genius, 137, 141-2.
Pretenders, Royal, 220-1.
Primacy in letters, 21-2, 42-3, 72 to 78, 152.
Proscenium boxes, 122.
Protestantism of England,163-4.
Prototype of Hamlet (Lecture 7th). Also (James I).

Q

Quadrilateral, The tragic, 37, 124.
Queen, The, an accessary? 181, 185, 195-6-7.
Quarto First, 107 to 112, 116, 119, 175-6, 185.
Quarto Second, 106 to 112, 116, 119, 125, 152 to 159.
"Queens of Scotland," 178.

R

Rapp, M., 91.

Reaction of guilt, 64-5.
Reasons for Revision, 119, 154, 158.
Recast of Hamlet, The final, 108, 119, 154, 157-8.
Regicide, 5, 23, 174 to 178, 199.
Remorse of Lady Macbeth, 44, 60, 63, 69.
Remorse of Macbeth, 69-70.
Representation, the poet's function, 93-4.
Resolution, Duty of, 104.
Responsibility, Human, 96-7-8.
Reticence of Macbeth, 61-2.
Revenge, Ethics of,188-9,190-1, 199, 200.
Revenge, The legacy of, 173, 189-190-1.
Reverent study, 24-5-6.
Richard II., 168.
Richard III., 78, 118.
Rizzio, 182, 184, 206.
Robert Elsmere, 95.
Roetschl, 90.
Rolfe, 31.
Rohrbach, 90.
Royal title, 62, 81, 84, 194 to 199.
Romeo and Juliet, 117-8.
Rosencrantz, 179, 182, 188, 218.
"Rye's England seen by foreigners," 203.

S

Sackville, Lord, 199.
Sanity, Hamlet's, 92-3, 111.
Sanity of genius, 132-3, 150.
Satan, a deceiver, 70.
Satan, Milton's, 58.
Saxo-Grammaticus, 178, 188, 192.
Scotland, its manners, 187 to 190.
Scotland, Macbeth's, 51-2.
Scotland visited by Shakespeare, 52, 187.
Scott, Sir Walter, 157.

INDEX.

Scott's, Sir Walter, James I., 201-2-3.
Scrope's, Baron, letter, 51-2.
"Second-best bed," 74.
Second Quarto, 106 to 112, 116, 119, 125, 152, 159.
Selfishness the essence of sin, 71.
Self-knowledge, 41-2.
Self-revelation, 148.
Self-reproach of Hamlet, 101-2, 191.
Self-estimate of Macbeth, 61.

SHAKESPEARE.
Ability, Transcendent, 43-4, 74 to 78, 100, 102, 131-2-3, 138, 150-1-2, 161-2, 177.
Ambition in Life, 156-7.
Arrival in London, 125, 127, 140.
Art, 99-100, 102, 140-1, 152, 161-2, 167, 190.
As an actor, 126-7-8, 140, 151.
Aspiration, 133, 150-1.
Attacks on him, 126 to 129.
Attorney's clerk. (See Noverint.)
Aversion to publication, 106, 109, 152-3.
"Beauties of Shakespeare," 23, 44.
Biographical Materials, 138-9, 143, 146 to 149, 150-1, 156-7.
Business talents, 148, 167.
Characterization of him, 118, 120, 126, 128-9.
Contemporary estimates, 118-19, 128-9, 133, 139, 149.
Contemptuous biography, 143, 146.
Courtier, A., 167-8, 177-8.
Creative faculty, 100, 102, 141, 150 to 153, 158.
Dramatic skill, 44, 50 to 53, 91-2, 98-9, 100, 141, 152, 190.
Early authorship, 115 to 144, 150, 176-7-8.
Early environment, 139, 143 to 146, 150 to 154, 163 to 170.
Education, 139, 143-4, 150 to 154.
Energy, 132-3.
Facility, 140.
Father of romantic drama, 134 to 139.
Fecundity, 140.
Genial temper, 129, 135, 140, 148.
Ideality, 189.
Inspiration to others, 22, 75, 76.
"Joannes Factotum," 128.
Learning, 144-5.
Legal phraseology, 144-5.
Literary primacy, 21 to 24, 42-3, 72 to 78, 152.
Manifoldness, 43, 72, 77-8, 102.
Metaphysics, 156, 165.
Method of composition, 151-2-3.
Moral vision, 58, 69-70-1, 74-5, 77, 91-2, 99-100, 167.
"Noverint," 126, 127, 129-130, 144-5, 151, 177.
Parallel with Bacon, 73.
Parallel with Marlowe, 125 to 129.
Parallel with Plutarch, 33.
Patriotism, 158-9, 165, 167-8, 177.
Patrons, 167-8, 170-1.
Permanence of influence, 22, 124, 149, 159.
Personality in Hamlet, His, 100 to 103, 154 to 157, 165.
Pessimism, 154 to 157.
Poetic skill, 141.
Popularity, 21.
Precocious genius, 141-2, 176-7.
Psychology, 44, 154 to 158.
Quasi universality, 43, 76-7-8, 102.

SHAKESPEARE (*Continued*).
  Rapid rise, 151.
  Reality of his characters, 43-4, 66-7, 74, 91-2, 103, 152, 186-7.
  Rhetoric, 23, 44, 141.
  Sanity of his genius, 132-3, 150.
  Skepticism, 95, 100, 155, 165.
  Supernaturalism, 53 to 60.
  Teachers, Alleged, 123, 138-9.
  "This Shakescene," 128.
  Visit to Scotland, 52, 187.
  Worth as a man, 129, 135, 148.
  Writings, where found, 26 to 29, 106 to 112, 116, 119, 125, 152, 159, 175-6, 185.
"Shakespeare as a lawyer," 127, 144.
"Shakespeare's Legal Acquirements," 127, 144.
"Shakespeare's Scholar," 25.
"Shakespeare, The footsteps of," 144.
SHAKESPEARIAN STUDY.
  Academic instruction, 29, 30 to 37.
  Advantages, 21, 22-3-4, 29, 36.
  Historical point of view, 30, 33 to 36.
  Method of study, 24, 29 to 37.
  Psychological study, 38-9-40, 44.
  Reverent study, 24-5-6.
Sidney, Sir Philip, 180.
Sievers, 90.
Significance of Hamlet. (See Lecture 3d.) Also 161-2.
Silberschlag, 180, 183-4.
Skepticism of Shakespeare, 95, 100, 155, 165.
Skepticism, 154, 163-4-5-6.
Skottowe, 120.
Smith, Wm. Henry, 142-3, 146.
Social conditions of Shakespeare's times, 188-9, 190.
Soliloquies, Hamlet's, 154-5, 207.

Soul-paralysis, 69, 95 to 99, 104.
Southampton, Earl of, 127, 171.
"Spanish tragedy, The," 120-1. 138.
Spirit of the age, 163, 165.
Spiritual symbolism, 53 to 60.
Stability of Shakespeare's influence, 22, 124, 149, 158-9
"Stationers' Register, The," 157, 175.
Staunton, 117.
Story, Wm. W., 56-7, 85, 155-6.
Strange, Lord, 140, 170.
"Strickland's Miss, Q. of Scotland," 178.
Study of Shakespeare. (See Shakespeare Study.)
Summary, Authorship of First Hamlet, 130-1.
Summary, Argument for prototype, 221-2.
Supernaturalism of Shakespeare, 53 to 60.
Sussex, Lord, 171.
Swinburne on Shakespeare's plays, 46.
Swinburne's apostrophe to Mary Stuart, 220.
Symonds, 120, 137.

T

Talents and genius, 33, 91-2, 131-2-3.
"Tamburlaine," 137-8.
"Taming of the Shrew," 117-8-9, 121.
Taylor, Nath'l W., 164.
Teachers, Shakespeare's alleged, 123, 138-9.
Tempest, The, 35, 37, 78.
Tests of genius, 131-2-3.
Text, Sacrifice of the, 214.
Text, verity of, 26 to 29, 106.
Thomas à-Kempis, 60.
Theories about Hamlet. (See Hamlet.)
Theory of Hamlet, Kentucky, 210.

INDEX.

Theory, Plumptre's, 180 to 186.
"Thirty years old," 182, 211 to 216.
Throckmorton, Sir Nicholas, 179, 217.
Time-Spirit, The, 163, 165.
Timmins, 116.
Title to throne, Claudius', 84, 194–5, 197–8–9.
"Titus Andronicus," 118, 144, 145.
Topography of Hamlet, 183, 186–7–8, 222.
Topography of Macbeth, 51.
"Tragedy of blood, The," 121, 151.
Tragic art, 37–8, 99, 100.
Tragic quadrilateral, 37, 124.
Travesty, Unconscious, 57, 89, 90.
"Truth, What is?" 163–4.
"Two Gentlemen of Verona." 118, 144, 145.

U

Unconsciousness of genius, 153.
Universality in literature, 43, 76–7–8, 102.
"University wits," 134–5–6.

V

Vacillation of Hamlet, 48, 94–5, 99.
Vacillation of Amiel, 96–7–8.

Venus and Adonis, 127, 140–1.
"Vicious Mole," 18.
Voltaire's criticism, 91.

W

Walsingham, 169, 171, 176, 205.
Warburton, 25.
Weldon, Sir A., 201–2.
Weever, 149.
Weird Sisters, The, 55–6, 58–9, 62–3.
Werder's Theory, 83–4, 90, 199.
Whipple, 40.
White, Richard Grant, 24 to 28, 40, 108, 177, 213.
Whole duty of man, 71.
Wilhelm Meister, quoted, 75–6, 80–1–2–3, 217–8.
Witches, 52, 54.
Withdrawal of Hamlet from stage, 108.
Will and Fate, 48, 59, 79, 82–3, 88, 92–3–4, 99, 100, 165, 190, 200.
"Wit's treasury," 118.
Wotton, Dr., 182.

Y

"Yorick, Poor," 212.

Z

Zimmerman, 186.